Praise for *12 1*

After reading the book, I have become much more aware of how selfish leadership can "slip" into employees and into the workplace culture. Selfish Leadership can end up causing significant harm if it is allowed to be accepted. Many people will likely recognize themselves in these situations and should consider whether they always speak up in time.

Peter Strand, Operations Director,
McDonald's Denmark

When I – as a leader – read the book, I am constantly reminded of the underlying responsibility leaders have for our employees - our behavior affects the whole person, not just their work life. The episodes described in the book are relevant and easily relatable to similar events throughout my career. I highly recommend the book because it inspires and motivates leaders to continue developing their own and the organization's leadership. A compelling narrative is combined with new theoretical examples and concrete tools.

Claus Jeppesen, People Director,
Legoland

This book can be read by everyone in an organization – to everyone's advantage. It provides a good insight into the personal development journey that the main character, Marie, goes through. I especially liked the focus on the "energy barometer" and the concrete tools that Marie is given to work with - they can be used both professionally and privately.

Karin Odum, Director of Global Marketing
and Branding at Novonesis

12

Tools for Managing a Selfish Leader

Library of Congress Control Number: 2024941051

ISBN (paperback): 978-1-963271-23-2
ISBN (Ebook): 978-1-963271-24-9

Armin Lear Press, Inc.
215 W Riverside Drive, #4362
Estes Park, CO 80517

12

Tools for Managing a Selfish Leader:

Unlocking Authenticity for Resilience

Josefine Campbell

CONTENTS

PREFACE

A blow against selfish leadership

It is quite by chance I hear it. I am just out shopping for a gift for my friend. When I reach the back of the shop to look on the shelves there, I hear through a half-open door to the back room an employee getting an old-fashioned reprimand from her boss. She has apparently forgotten something important, and although she makes apologies several times, it does not reduce the shouting.

To me, it sounds like a boss reacting impulsively, fallen prey to the situation. I look around the shop. It seems I am the only person hearing it. On the spot, I do not know what I should do, as I am only out shopping on my day off. Later when I finally make my choice of a gift, the very same seller, red-eyed, receives my payment. She has no courage to look me or anyone else in the face and her movements are quite mechanical. It is obvious that she is feeling fragile.

However, when I go out of the door, I know exactly what I need to do, as my work is with leadership. This is not at all the first time I overhear or witness selfish leadership. In addition, what consequences it has for people the employees – and as well for the leaders. It can make people feeling like they cannot succeed in life. They loose themselves. However right now as I leave the shop, it seems obvious I must make use of this knowledge.

This book is intended for all who are leaders or who work under a leader. Although Marie, whom you will meet in the book, is a middle manager, it could just as well be your own self or someone you care for in the predicament she encounters in this story. You do not need to be a boss to understand Marie's situation and what it feels to lose yourself.

Most places of work are not for children. This statement applies in both a literal and a metaphorical sense. Many clever and hard-working people suffer relatively many bruises at their work. In this context, we don't mean it's because of the physical work they do. These are the invisible bruises caused by words and actions that weigh heavy on the employee. Many designate them as politics. When these "politicians" grow egocentric, manipulating, and overstep their limits, they are guilty of what I call selfish leadership.

It is important that employees place a basic trust in their leader, and it is nice if they possess a liking for one another. However, leadership is not a contest to win popularity. Sometimes a leader has to make a difficult decision or disclose unpopular facts. However, there is a difference between a consistent leadership, which can also handle in a selfish manner, and what I denote as selfish leadership.

Within consistent leadership, a leader can appear to act selfish, when he comes with news about a tough situation, but he gives this information and implements it in a manner in keeping with good principles like responsibility, propriety, or respect.

Selfish leadership is evident when a leader consciously or unconsciously uses manipulative methods, bypasses personal limits, and exhibits egoism in whatever manner they like. Sometimes the reason for this is a lack of conscience and empathy, and sometimes their behavior is the product of unconscious, immature habits. When I use the word immature, I do not infer that age is a parameter, since the matter has nothing to do with how old they are. It is a matter of shouldering responsibility for our actions and developing ourselves when we receive relevant feedback. We never grow too old to change for the better. Brain research shows we can create new neural connections between the synapses in our brain – during the whole of our life.

The matter we are discussing here is that employees, like the shop attendant, can receive unacceptable treatment. Her treatment exceeds the limit. Her personal requirements do not receive due respect.

In Marie's case, her boss yelled at her and sometimes manipulated her, placing her in detracting situations.

Some people break down from stress, when subjected to selfish leadership. Others subjected to this form of leadership, manage to survive, just like Marie. However, they use up large amounts of their energy doing so – is this really the way we want them to spend their energy?

Marie is a middle manager, and she both has a boss and she is a boss herself. When Marie's boss makes use of selfish leadership, which Marie's boss Martin does, she functions as a buffer, to keep the brunt of his selfish leadership methods from impinging on her own employees. To function as a middle manager can be one of the most demanding roles in a company. Middle managers can face enormous challenges, often threatening them on several fronts. Therefore, we ought to nurture good leaders at every level.

Good leaders play an enormously important role in our society. Good leaders give others growth potential. Without good middle leaders, many things would not have coherency – and a lot could not take place. We are lucky that some grow to be leaders.

The great drawback is that selfish leadership has won acceptance on social levels, *implying its inevitability.* When we deal with leaders, we find many places an unwritten code, saying you have to put up with the heat in the kitchen. In large organizations, top-level leaders have either learned to co-exist with selfish leadership, or they have been so incredibly fortunate to have been spared from it, though my experience shows this to be the case for only a tiny fraction - if at all so.

There is without doubt improvement in sight. Nevertheless, many leaders forget how it is when working at a lower level in the organizations. Changes do not take place of their own accord – if we assess the increases in stress, depression and exhaustion, changes cannot come fast enough.

In this book, you will get a chance to sit in the manner of a fly on a wall and witness stages of development normally kept confidential. The journey tell about a true happening. The central figure in Marie's tale wants her story to gain publicity to help others unlocking their authenticity for resilience - like she did. I have made up an analogous story, altering many of the details, but in which I have maintained the overriding moral – the consequences it can have for the employee to have been subjected to a selfish leadership. Marie receives coaching and you get to know what happens during her coaching. The coaching processes can appear to be very different and have very different focus and content. They are not always as dramatic as in Marie's case. Most people come because they want to improve and pass on further to the next stage. It is important to remember that all progress is individual. Marie's case itself is somewhat artificial, as focus is on demonstrating the tools rather than on presenting a true-life copy of Marie's progress.

As a coach for leaders, I become not seldom a confidante for their difficult problems. These can be things that are so painful or embarrassing that they have never told them before or can relate to a great joy too intimate to share with others or because there are not many people who can understand.

However, we often discuss quite usual leadership challenges, such as how we can derive more benefit from our meetings, how we can deal with an especially difficult employee, colleague or boss, how we can achieve promotion in our jobs, how we can realize our true value more fully or how we can handle stress and replenish our everyday energy.

Although these challenges are quite ordinary, they are not topics we normally discuss with others. Either because our friends do not possess a true understanding of our daily activities – or because we feel an uncertainty and a lack of confidence, which makes discussion difficult. My work allows me insight into the challenges many successful leaders really grapple with. An insight only few manage to get. Yet, it's an insight I feel all employees at a place of work ought to possess. Both to take proper care of ourselves and in togetherness to change the conditions.

Conditions need to improve somewhat at our places of work – and this can indeed take place in a large majority of cases, so we can fulfill our tasks satisfactorily as required, without paying a price with blood, sweat and tears. To quash any unacceptable ideas about what we must tolerate and what behavior is acceptable at our workplace, we need to establish an unequivocal dialogue.

I hope you will like reading my book and you will join in creating a better workday for all of us.

ONE

Marie's collapse

X-Corp headquarters is located in brand new buildings, enjoying a proximity to the harbor and surrounded by small bushes, that were yet not full-grown. You could still glimpse traces from the architect's blueprint with its drawings of people in seated positions or strolling in the small green oases adorned with benches placed at intervals in front of the large entrance to X-Corp.

Marie could still remember the day she came here for her first job interview. X-Corp had recently removed to these premises, although their renovation was yet not fully complete. Building workers and machinery stood in many places, and U2 was playing on the radio. Just loud enough to enable Marie to hum with the pop music that filled the building site. The entrance was finished, and it looked impressive with its large stairway leading up to large glass doors, behind which the head of a reception clerk was visible as she sat behind a broad and ample counter.

To Marie it felt like a dream to work here. Right from her days at business school. X-Corp had a very good reputation, offered many avenues for a career, chances for promotion and a good reference to have on one's resume. Many applied and few passed through the needle's eye after their many tests.

That day she was ready and felt the time was now. She had received the right education, the right amount of work experience, and she possessed good references. She knew she was skilled at her work – and she could do more than required. It was a self-sure and competent Marie, who spoke politely to the receptionist, informing she had a job interview with Martin and Alfred from the products department. And she got the job.

Marie and her team have quarters on the 3rd floor in proximity with the other product teams in X-Corp. They form part of a large, open office landscape, each team sitting by themselves in a group. After Marie's promotion as a product manager a couple of years ago, she now has her own office next to her boss, Martin, who is the boss for all the product managers. All the floors in the building resemble each other essentially. The large office landscapes, the plants in plastic pots supplied by a private firm that comes every week to water them, the small pantries distributed at set locations on each floor, with a sink, a small kitchen table and a big coffee-brewer, that can produce anything from coffee to bouillon soup. In addition, there are one-man offices down near the giant staircase connecting all the floors and as well a large number of meeting rooms. All with walls of glass.

Today, Marie has an important meeting with Martin, who is the leader placed directly above her, and his boss Alfred, and this takes up all her thoughts.

Marie stands talking to Thomas, her most entrusted subordinate, when Martin and Alfred come towards her at the time appointed for the meeting. "Are you ready, Marie?" Alfred asks in a friendly manner.

Thomas greets the two men, and Marie answers them a little too coolly. "Bet your life. I'm ready."

Neither of the two men says anything. They walk into the meeting room together, and Martin seats himself beside Alfred, so that they sit side by side at the long end, and Marie can only do likewise opposite. Alone.

Two against one, not the best way to start the meeting, Marie thinks, why did she not anticipate this happening – and perhaps gone in a couple of minutes before the meeting and could steer it from the beginning. Martin starts the ball rolling right away, thumps his papers down on the table and looks at Marie directly." "Yes, Marie, I have summoned this meeting and brought Alfred along, because I feel we need to have a talk about your present big project, Blue Wonder, which has not quite shown the progress we anticipated. We are only having this talk to see if we can help you in some way, so that we can bring it *back on track*," Martin uses the tone of voice he reserves for when Alfred is nearby.

"I am glad to hear that," Marie clears her throat. She can feel an itching sensation under her shirt collar, and her mouth suddenly feels dry, "I have had the same thought, to assess the progress of the project together with you both."

"Excellent," Martin says. "So, far, so good. Will you start by giving us a run-through of the project from beginning to end – and especially with focus on the status right now, and what you have had of thoughts during the last sprint?"

"Of course," Marie answers and takes a deep breath, as she starts sharing pages out. "As you can see on page 1, where I have shown the original production plan, budget and prognosis as compared with the modified production plan, revised budget, and prognosis, you can see we unfortunately have a number of deviations. I intend to discuss them one by one. Number 1…"

"Marie, I am forced to stop you here. These numbers are completely new to me…"

Marie's blush has begun to work its way up her throat from the collar of her shirt.

"It was these numbers I showed you last week in your office. Do you not remember, I came to your work-desk, and we examined the figures – you remained seated, and I was standing?" Marie turns her head quickly to one side, and then the other and looks at Martin with a forced smile.

"Me sitting and you standing?" Martin lets the question hang a little in mid-air. "I think I would have remembered that." Martin smiles at her with a cold but friendly smile.

"But I did, you said too that that was what happens, and we should talk about it this week…" Marie looks helplessly at Martin.

Oh, she can hear she is already on the defensive and giving importance to unimportant details. Get a grip on yourself, Marie, she whispers silently to herself.

Martin just looks at Marie. Alfred interrupts.

"It is not an important matter, who stood where, Marie. Please continue the review."

Marie takes a deep breath, presses her lips together, trying hard to retain her composure. She feels she is quivering and looks down at her hands but cannot see they are shaking. The meeting is progressing in no way as she had planned – or discussed with her husband David.

"Yes, but as I said in item 1, so…"

"I am forced to interrupt you once more," Martin says, now with a hard tone in his voice. He does not conceal it, at any rate. "I am reading ahead while sitting here, since I have not seen these figures before…"

"Yes, you have, Martin, stop it," Marie says in a weak voice.

Martin lifts up his hand. Marie's red suffusion has now reached up to her chin.

"If only you will let me finish speaking, Marie," Martin says now with a distinctly hard and sharp tone. "I cannot understand why your prognosis does not show modifications of the first prognosis for the months ahead. Now when the project has fared so badly, as it has in fact done. That we have to confess." Martin looks at Alfred and shrugs his shoulders as if to soften up his hard demeanor.

"That is the reason for this meeting today. To be honest, Marie, we just can't seem to recognize your trademark here."

Martin and Alfred scrutinize Marie in the same way. Two against one, Marie again thinks. However, Martin does not stop.

"I need to be honest about the figures you are showing us today for the first time. It boggles me that these figures don't vary. It seems a little mystic." Martin looks her in the face, picks up the paper to emphasize his amazement, turning his gaze to see if Alfred is still backing him up, which the latter quite obviously does. Alfred for sure is in agreement with him. Martin looks at Marie again, with his head tilted.

"Yes, but I have calculated them. Thomas too has calculated them, they are accurate enough…"

"You have not even adjusted them a single cent up or down, it can't be right," Martin is unrelenting. "Not a single cent for even one item, these figures are exactly the same from start to finish for the next couple of months, I can see." Martin waves the paper now.

"There are statutory procedures in the firm that apply the first three months, and we are extremely well acquainted with them from the other big projects we have had. They always lead to a good result. You know that, Martin," Marie says, now rather too vigorously, which she can hear, as the words leave her mouth.

Marie can almost not draw a breath. She can feel anger rising in her, but worse than that, she can also feel tears threatening. However, she must not cry. Nor scream… everything seems to be spinning around.

"I am positively sure you just cannot do calculations in that manner, Marie. Every project always needs a separate assessment every time. That can perhaps also explain why this project has progressed the way it has done. If that is your approach."

Marie stares open-mouthed at Martin and then at Alfred. She just looks at them.

Alfred says nothing. As usual, he says nothing. The whole matter seems so surrealist, and she feels dizzy, thirsty and places a hand on her throat. She feels an itching. It itches again, and then tears well out of her. She cannot restrain her tears, though she knows well it is not acceptable to sit crying at a meeting with both Alfred and Martin present. However, she cannot keep her tears in. The whole matter can just go to hell. It is as if the stress from the months past have loosened their grip and flow out with her tears, and she just gives up all worries, her thoughts about what is up and what is down, about Martin's behavior, and about her own situation and what she can do. She can endure no more. She is no longer the same Marie she has been before. Alfred clears his throat and finally says something.

"Marie, I can see you react a little too strongly now. I feel we must adjourn the meeting, so you can compose yourself, and we can take the matter up again next week, and I would ask you to calculate the prognosis just one more time."

Marie just looks at Alfred with blank eyes…calculate…one more time…but the calculations are right, this is the normal procedure, her thoughts race wildly, but at the end she nods acceptance. She gets to her feet and leaves the meeting room quickly without saying a word. She does not look at Martin, and she begins to cry. Covering her face with her hands, she walks hurriedly towards the toilets. She does not look up. She wants only to know that no one has knowledge of what transpired in the room. She can simply not overcome the thought of it now. What are all her colleagues thinking about her now?

The start of the day had been rather different. It had started filled with hope.

"Perhaps it's time you stand up for yourself in a proper way against Martin. Especially when Alfred is present. That will let him see, what you have to fight against." It is David, Marie's husband of many years, who is talking. Marie and David are standing in the kitchen, each with his coffee cup, and discuss Marie's coming meeting with Martin and Alfred. Martin has a number of product managers under him, but Marie is the product manager for their biggest and most selling portfolio, and she does a good job. Or rather did it well. The last couple of months has shown a recession. She cannot really find an explanation. She has woken up with a pain in her stomach. Again.

"It's not so easy. I have tried, but every time he ensnares me using some technical detail that is not relevant, but which is too specialized for others to easily understand, or he can make it look in a roundabout way, that I am lying, so I stop trying or I give a poor answer, which makes it look as if it is he who is right." Marie sighs.

"He is extremely well versed and intelligent – and quick off the mark in situations of this kind. I have never won over him in this kind of discussion."

"But you too are clever, Marie, and Alfred must be able to see that. Think what you have achieved the last couple of years in X-Corp. You have proved time and again that you too are extremely capable, and you often spot eventualities before all others. That you are so astute has saved you many times. Yes, it is only ONE project that has been derailed – just one time, but it is not on account of your lacking ability, but because Martin keeps changing his mind and he puts burdens on you, the way he acts."

"I know, but Alfred considers Martin to be his shining star – the rest of us cannot reach as high. He always ends up saying Martin is right, and the rest of us must conform and take the blame."

"You must make another try. You have in fact a chance today to open Alfred's eyes. The three of you don't meet so often," David continues. Marie nods in assent and gazes at her feet. David goes towards her and cuddles her in his arms.

"I am not after you. I hope you know that my darling."

Marie nods silently in David's arms. It is nice to feel a hug now. But when was it that she had started feeling so tiny, so helpless, sad and incapable?

"It's not easy for us to see you burying yourself away, as you have been doing for the past couple of months. You are irritable, distraught and tired. You are not able to fall asleep at night. When did you last get a really good night's sleep – or gone for the walks you love to take?"

David holds Marie in front of him and looks her in the eyes. "You know the children and I love you so much, but we miss having our glad, strong Marie. Work is not everything," David continues.

"I know that. I love you dearly too, that you know. Only I can't find head or tail with things anymore. I no longer know what's right and what's wrong, and you of all people know I normally can," Marie says. Now it is David, who nods. He holds on to Marie's shoulders.

"Some days I feel the whole blame rests on Martin's shoulders. He is simply so irrational and beyond the pale of reason. On other days, I feel doubt, as to whether, it might be me, who is wrong. Some days Martin is so inspiring to work together with and he finds the most ingenious solutions, and he listens and gives support. I have grown older too, and perhaps that is the reason, why I cannot keep up with the others anymore," Marie has an apologetic smile as she looks up at David.

"Stop that. You are not at risk of falling off, you must just stand up to Martin and you must do so today. Yes, you can. You are a shining star too and you must put Martin in his place now. Alfred has to show his own mettle. You are not the first product manager that has given up in working with Martin – regardless of how charismatic he sometimes appears," David says, giving Marie a nudge.

"You're right. I must tell my own version of the true story today, win or lose," Marie says.

"That's the spirit. I stand behind you, if you need me," David gives her an encouraging smile.

When Marie goes back to work, she has a feeling that she has not experienced a long time. She has faith in this feeling. The last two months there has been a struggle. The last project has been completely derailed. This has never happened to her before, and she does not know, how she has ended here. She has achieved many things in her lifetime, someone has told her so, she is clever, she has achieved good results, and she is intelligent. Results have confirmed this many times since she completed her studies. The last couple of years have been corroborated by the intelligence tests she took at Corp X at the time of her offer of a job and at the time of her promotion to be products leader. She knows she is a good leader. She always has a high score in the well-being surveys, and she has many employees who have remained with her for many years. She gives really a lot of importance to this and keeps it in focus at all times. She knows she is nothing without her motivated employees. She would not be able to achieve the results she in fact enjoys without their support.

Nevertheless, she cannot find an explanation for her situation. She has an intuitive feeling that it can have relation to Martin, but it feels a weak excuse to give your boss the whole blame why you suddenly cannot perform your work normally. She has seen and heard some of the other product managers use this excuse a few months earlier, and they don't work for the concern any longer. However, Martin has made it more difficult than usual to run this last project. That was what she would bring up today at the meeting with Alfred and Martin, so they could themselves find a solution for how to continue. The project must be a success.

Marie runs to the toilet at the back, hurries inside, shuts the door and sinks noiselessly to the floor, where she keeps sitting with her hands around her legs, and bursts again into tears. She feels as if she does not know her own self. She finds her telephone and rings to David.

"Hello, darling. How did the meeting go? Did you say no to them?" David asks her with warm interest. Marie only keeps crying in the telephone.

"What has happened to you?" David asks now with obvious concern.

Marie hiccups her way through the whole story. David listens, asks questions and they conclude that it was of course not optimal, and she ought to get hold of Alfred and afterwards Martin and make excuses and give an explanation that she feels stressed but that she will come up to tops again. Marie is embarrassed and full of shame. The whole matter feels so uncomfortable, which she says to David several times in the course of their conversation. Her conversation with David works like a cold shower and Marie decides to find Alfred first. The job she has here is the job she has dreamed about and now she must make a fight. She can fight and fight she will.

Marie finds Alfred who looks as if he is on his way out to buy lunch. He looks at her a trifle impatiently as she just manages to accost him with his jacket on.

"Yes, what's the matter now, Marie?" he says a little hard, but quickly changes his tone. "Do you feel better?" Alfred asks insincerely.

"I would just like to say I'm sorry and apologize for my behavior at the meeting today, Alfred. It was of course out of place, and it won't happen again."

Alfred looks at her and gives a quick smile.

"You have been with us a good while, Marie, and done a good job until now. We would not like to lose you," Alfred begins to speak.

Marie feels her head is spinning – have they already begun on the procedure of firing her because of a *single* unsuccessful project?

"I spoke with Martin after our meeting, and we know you are a clever person, and that many years of experience and meticulous work have given you more than just ordinary skills within your specialized field."

Marie nods and stammers a few words of thanks.

Alfred continues: "And you are extremely good at working together with your team as well. You are normally good at cooperating and if anyone can, you can make any employee blossom up under your guidance. So much so, that even the employees others give up as hopeless, and would otherwise be dropouts, become key associates after they have been under your leadership for some time. You know your business, both technically and as a leader. The worst we can say about you perhaps is you are a little too openhearted for a leader at your level – at least in Corp X, where corporate politics is as big part of work life as it is in any other multi-international corporation.

Marie hears only the words "you are normally" and "a little too openhearted" resounding inside her head. Are they going to fire her? Marie can no longer keep matters chin up.

Susanne, the HR-Director in Corp X, rings straight away to their favorite coach Caroline, after talking with Alfred. Fortunately, Caroline answers the telephone. Susanne informs Caroline that they have an employee who had a nervous breakdown crying in a meeting with Alfred, and they have already decided, it could be a good idea for Marie to have some talks with Caroline. Marie has already agreed.

"It could be even better, if I could get a talk with Martin,"

Caroline says. "Do you think we can get him to do so this time – he is Marie's direct manager?"

"It sounds an obvious idea, if we can get him to agree. His leadership style is creating some problems," Susanne says. "He has eluded us the previous times. However, I will try again to get at him. I promise."

Susanne lays the phone down, sighs audibly and says quietly to herself, "What a mess."

"Are you ok?" asks Helena, Susanne's closest employee.

"I don't know. They just telephoned from the products department. Martin has again been treating an employee too hard. I have just hung up on the telephone after talking with Caroline. It is not easy, when the matter concerns Martin, but you know that too. Every time, I tell Alfred, he needs perhaps to get some leadership training, he just answers saying that I must solve the problem, because he cannot do without Martin. Neither can we, in fact."

"That's not true, Helena says with hopelessness in her voice.

"How many employees can they afford to lose because of Martin, so…"

"Yes, that's just it," Susanne says thoughtfully.

"Who is it this time?" Helena asks.

"It's Marie, and she is simply one of the best. We can't afford to lose her."

TWO

The signals sound

A couple of days later Marie gets a lift to Caroline's office. By David. She was not in a condition to drive herself. Quite suddenly, she could not manage to find the car keys, go out to the car and drive to Caroline's office at the other end of the town. Even just taking a shower this morning required a giant effort and David had noticed it. He postponed his first meeting that day to drive her. They said nothing in the car.

Marie just sat looking at all the people in the morning traffic. They were all in such a hurry, she thought, and they looked the way they normally did, as everything did, as usual. Here she sat looking at them, all living their lives, and at that moment, she doubted she would ever once more become one of them. Those on their way.

Caroline comes to meet Marie, bids her welcome and shows her in. They will be sitting in a cozy, dimly lit oblong room with a long conference table in the middle and red chairs around it. It has the appearance of a meeting room, Marie thinks. Over the table hangs an oblong silver lamp, resembling some or other organic sculpture. Marie seems to lose concentration, which Caroline notices and she explains to her.

"This is my husband's design. He is a designer. We both use this meeting room," Caroline says, pointing at the two meeting chairs standing at the back of the room, near to a pile of blank paper sheets, a pen, two glasses, and a pitcher with water. "I have made ready for the two of us here."

Marie nods and looks at the whiteboard hanging beside her. She just cannot make a choice.

"Sit just where you like," Caroline says with a smile."

Marie takes a seat and raises her gaze to Caroline. "Is it ok if I sit here?" Marie asks with lack of sureness.

"Yes, you can just sit, where you want to sit," Caroline continues.

"Hmm," Marie says and looks down at her hands.

Caroline gives Marie an introduction as to how her process can develop, and an excerpt of what Caroline at one time says, that Marie could afterwards remember, is that Marie is not at all the first leader to sit in the selfsame chair Marie chose – also after facing challenges.

" Your P&C-partner Susanne has telephoned and she sketched roughly the events that have taken place, but shall we not begin by you telling me about the incident, and your feelings about what happened," Caroline says.

Marie consents. Everything goes well while Marie tells about what she does, her tasks at work, her career and education, but when she reaches the day when she had a meeting with Martin and Alfred, she can remember only small fragments. She can remember when Martin interrupted her, when in tears she telephoned David, and with a last fragment of memory, being on the top floor with Alfred. Caroline nods and straightens her oversize glasses a trifle.

"Marie," she says, after Marie again sits down and stares at her hands. "We will solve this matter, and I can definitely help you, but we must first determine the state you are in right now. Are you ready?"

Now it is Marie's turn to nod in assent. "I am prepared to seek help, since I don't really understand what is happening inside me right now. All of a sudden it has grown so difficult for me to go to work," she says at last.

"I do understand you," Caroline says "and we shall restore and bring back the joy in your work. However first, we must begin with you – and we shall progress little by little until we complete the whole process. Let us begin with how you feel right now. I have printed this list for you as it gives an overview of a number of bodily signs. I would like you to sit now and mark off those you feel you have," Caroline says, handing out this page:

1st Tool: Stress signals

Please tick off the ones you feel.

Body signals:

O Headache

O Throbbing heartbeat

O High blood pressure

O Trembling hands

O Bodily restlessness

O Tensions and pains

O Shallow breathing

O Pressure on chest

O Sleeplesness or interrupted sleep

O Prickly feeling on hands and legs

O Dizziness
O Sucking feeling
O Stomach pains
O Diarrhea

O Reduced sex drive
O Lack of appetite
O Worsening of
   chronic illness

Emotions:

O Feeling threatened
O Stressed
O Vulnerable to criticism
O Feeling of guilt – bad
   conscience
O Feeling of incompetence
O Low self-confidence

O Nervous
O Lonely
O Aggressive, frustrated,
   irritable or restless
O Distraught
O Tired feeling
O Sadness

Behavior:

O Do you go to extremes?
O Increased/Reduced appetite
O Increased alcohol
   consumption
O Frequent/more frequent
   tobacco smoking
O Increased use of medicine
O Reduced desire for company
   (at work and at home)
O Unstable moods
O Nervousness
O Impulsiveness
O Nervous laughter

O Do you have difficulty in
   making a decision?
O Unstable
O Reduced performance level
O Minor conflicts with
   colleagues
O Increased sick leave
O Have you begun to be
   slipshod?
O Frequent physical
   complaints
O Are you out of sorts?
O Lack of humor

Marie takes the sheet of paper and begins to tick off. Many ticks. She surprises herself at how many ticks she marks. She is not at all aware of how serious her condition is. When did it begin, she asks herself many times and why have I not seen it?

When did she begin feeling headaches, heart throbbing, restlessness in her body, insomnia, a sinking feeling in her stomach? When did David and she last have sex? And now that it appears in black and white, she realizes she often feels she is being threatened, pressed, constantly pressed, in fact she cannot tolerate criticism any more, and she reacts at the tiniest provocation, and often she feels sad.

When she arrives at the last heading on the subject of behavior, she starts to cry. She has begun making mistakes. The last big project is a clear example, showing she has made mistakes. She has had difficulty in making decisions, although she has never had this problem before.

She has always had great confidence in herself at her work. Without her hands shaking. She looks down at her hands. They are trembling now. All the ticks she marked are blinking. The signals she has disregarded for so long are sounding so loud, that the noise is unbearable.

"I find the exercise a little difficult," Marie says somewhat apologetically.

"I understand that well," Caroline says, paying her great attention.

"It is not difficult to answer in this manner, but I feel sorry when I see how bad my situation is. Just look at how many ticks I have marked," Marie answers quietly.

Caroline takes the paper and runs her eyes down the list. "I make use of this list with body signals because it helps us both to really understand how you feel. It can help us have an overview of what you need to be observant of, when your body produces excess cortisol and adrenaline, because you have too much stress. The neuro-chemical process that takes place in your brain and in your body is the same. However, its degree can be more or less serious.

The signals can be short-lived, like when you feel sweat in the palms of your hands and you get an ache in your stomach in the eve of an important event, or long-lived, like in your case now, after suffering from bad sleep and irritation for several weeks. If matters get worse, you need of course to see a doctor," Caroline explains.

They discuss at length all Marie symptoms, and on completing, Marie marks additional ticks on the list. This is the first time in a long while that Marie indulges in thinking about her true condition, and when she sees all the ticks on the paper, she realizes it is high time to bring about a change. How could she have let matters reach this far? She sighs.

"I am one of the people going down with stress or what?" Marie suddenly says aloud. Perhaps directed mostly to herself.

Caroline looks at Marie and hands her a new page. "This is a model of my version of the stress ladder. I don't know if you have heard of it?" Caroline asks.

"Vaguely," Marie answers

2nd Tool: Stress staircase

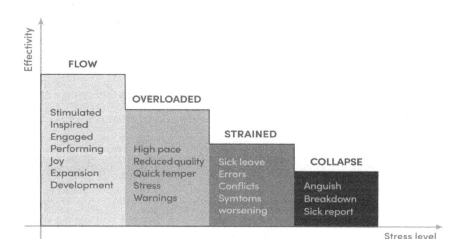

Figure 1. Stress Staircase©, Josefine Campbell, 2024.[1]

"The stress staircase is a useful tool to enable a bird's eye view of the different stages you can arrive at, and follow your development from being well-functioning to being in a state of dangerous stress. The stress ladder depicts four stages, matching my own matrix, which we will discuss more the next time. Every step you go down, the stress symptoms grow more pronounced, and your work capabilities lessen. The four steps are *in flow, overloaded strained and collapse.* Each stage has its own hallmark, which you must be on a careful lookout for. I feel we ought now to review them."

Marie sits and stares at the paper, her hands resting on her

---

1   The Stress staircase is developed with an outset in the work by Marie Kingston and Malene Friis in their book from 2016; Stop Stress – håndbog for ledere, with the English title; Stop Stress, a Managers Handbook, and the work by Majken Matzau in her book from 2014; Rigtige mænd går også i sort, with the English title; Real Men get Black-Outs too

thighs, and she contemplates the stress ladder with an empty look in her eyes. Marie clears her throat.

"It is not difficult to see where I am," she says looking at the table.

"Where do you think you are?" Caroline asks.

"I am in strained'. I cannot understand at all why I didn't see it. Before it was too late, before 1 apparently lost control at my work."

Caroline gives Marie an intense and warm look.

"I cried. In front of Alfred. Oh, how embarrassing this is. In front of Alfred, come on, Marie."

"That is quite ok, Marie. There were many good reasons. "My recommendation is you begin to have focus on saving your personal energy. What gives you energy? For some people, it is a walk in green natural surroundings, for others it is a ride on a motorbike, to work with crochet, to go for a small run, to practice meditation, to laugh with friends, hug loved ones, eat healthy food or cook food for others. When you have a lot of energy, you can feel a great platitude – in fact, we can just denote it as platitude. You have need of energy and platitude, in order to restore your brain and your nervous system, but we can talk much more about that next time. When I talk about energy here, I do not mean energy of the kind that you accumulate. You need instead just to reduce speed now."

Caroline looks at Marie. "Do you need me to talk with Susanne about you, or will you talk with her yourself? You must know that our conversations are held confidential, and I can narrate only what you would have me talk about," Caroline says and straightens her large spectacles up again. "Are you okay with this, does it sound like a good plan for you?"

"It sounds okay and the best I can do right now. You can tell Susanne so," Marie says. "It is what I have recommended to my other colleagues too, who have worked under Martin, when he gives them a hard time. To listen to what you tell them."

Marie is smiling for the first time.

"That sounds good, and we must talk about Martin too, but we'll do that first after you have regained your legs," Caroline says and smiles at her.

"That sounds good," Marie says.

THREE

Mental surf

Monday morning Marie is sitting at Caroline's meeting table again.

"How do you feel today? Caroline asks, after they sat and talked for a while.

"Yes, a little better, but I still find it somewhat of a trial to go to work. I find it rather embarrassing, but it's ok. I don't know if the others saw me crying, and Martin has given me a little peace, so it's okay," Marie says with a twinkle in her eye that quickly vanishes again.

"Then you manage to relax a little?" Caroline asks.

"Yes, I try. However, it's not easy. I am used to being active all the time, so I feel somewhat at a loose end. However, I give higher priority to my sleep, and I have begun going for walks, three times daily, with our dog Jax. Some afternoons when I come home from work, we go for very long walks. I really enjoy them, and this gives me energy," Marie says and gives a sideways look at Caroline.

"That's a good thing. That is the way it must be. It is quite normal to find it difficult to relax. Your nervous system is in a state of alarm. You have been overburdened. That wears you down. The fact that you can feel it is just an indication that your condition is improving. That's progress – even though it may not feel like that right now. We made it clear to Susanne at our last meeting that you must be free from stress, and that I have stipulated very categorically. They were definitely in agreement, and that is why Martin has left you alone," Caroline answers. "Everything is as it ought to be."

"That is not completely true. Martin has sent me an SMS a couple of times outside of office hours, and I have of course replied," Marie says. Her face changes colour. It becomes more white.

"That you don't need to. I am sorry to hear that Martin cannot fully respect our agreement with Susanne, but shall I not talk about it with her? – and perhaps I should talk with him directly?"

Marie gives a nod. "Yes, please do so. It is not because I am unwilling, but I just feel it is not easy right now."

"Yes, I'll do so when we finish talking."

Marie gives a smile. "Thank you, Caroline."

Caroline begins to repeat briefly, what they talked about last, and she explains what they will talk about today following up on the last meeting. The last time we did damage control. The aim of that session was to create as much calm as possible about your situation so we can improve your state. Today we will delve a little deeper into your situation to obtain an overview. I will give you my opinion about what a good program for you could look like, and we will forward it to Susanne, so she can follow on the sideline as a witness.

Afterwards, I can have a talk with her and come to an agreement. The two of us must agree completely to what I will tell her, since our conversation is confidential. However, first, I will make you familiar with a matrix that perhaps can give you a critical view on your situation, and the matters bringing you here. Does this sound like a good plan? Caroline goes to the whiteboard and starts drawing this matrix:

3rd Tool: The awareness matrix

Fig. 2: The awareness matrix©, Campbell (2023).

"The awareness matrix has four boxes. It represents four states of mind, which I just now have drawn on the whiteboard, and they show the four extreme mental states. They are *Narrow, Fragile, Mellow* and *Agile*. I will discuss them one after another. When you are in the *Narrow* state, you can be very productive and complete tasks you have postponed. You are in a focused state of mind. However, you do not have a wide perspective, and you are not flexible or open to new ideas.

When you are in this state because your brain thinks you are in a situation critical for your survival. The result of this is that your ability to analyze, gain perspective, and think logically and creatively become less. As well, your brain pumps the stress hormones cortisol, adrenaline, and noradrenaline out in your body, exerting a high toll on your energy resources. Many people live alternating constantly between *narrow* and *fragile*. It is exhausting."

Marie gives a nod. She feels she has been living and working like this now for a long time.

"You use up much more energy, when you are either *narrow* or *fragile* in the left zone in the matrix, than when you are in the right zone," Caroline says. "You consume energy non-sustainably. Just as if you drive your car badly, and quickly use a large amount of petrol. When I drive well, an eco-lamp in my car lights up. what we talk about, is the opposite since personal energy is your gasoline. There are limits for how long your brain and nervous system can endure that. It wears you out. This means you cannot think clearly and become more easily subject to stress, overwhelmed, or overcome. Individuals, who are gifted and are an asset, can become a heavy burden for a team, if they for the most part are fragile. Not only can you feel yourself very drained, when you are fragile, but you can also drain others. This is worth remembering. On the other hand, when we are agile, and it is in this category we all want to belong, then we freely can contribute to our impressions of our surroundings, and to how we will respond to them. For there are many perspective views and you will be in a mental state where you can see many perspectives. You will also be in a better condition to exercise creativity, think logically, understand others and absorb new impressions. You will feel a personal surplus, and you will be able to make conscious decisions on how to act, instead of letting an automatic program direct your brain and body.

There is where we need to have you. On the other hand, when you are mellow, you can in fact be ready, but your energy is at a low level. You can be calm and relaxed, but you do not possess great energy. Perhaps you are a little subdued and retiring, or perhaps you just let yourself flow along – all depending on your temperament. In this condition, you can restitute yourself, replenish your energy and renew your strength. There is nothing stigmatic or detrimental with tiredness. So long as you remember to recharge your energy. Otherwise, you will revert to a worn-out condition."

Marie sits listening, sometimes she appears distant, other times she seems moved, but Caroline does not feel at any time that she is not in contact with her. Caroline now feels she can proceed to the next stage with Marie." As we discussed last time, you stood on the rung *strained* on the stress ladder."

"Yes, and I have been in the narrow and fragile states of mind too much, am I not?" Marie says, not making it sound like a question.

"That's right – and this is normal, after having been under a selfish leadership for a long period of time," Caroline says with sympathy and explains. "The principal axes in the model depict whether you have high energy or low energy, whether you are ready or hijacked.

On a normal day of work, we surf around between different mental states. We can shuffle around between the four boxes, without it resulting in our demise with stress, but we must the whole time be aware of where we are and how long time we stay.

Sometimes you are ready mentally, and you perform with your maximum ease. When you are ready, you are in a better condition to cooperate, lead, understand, make right decisions, make changes and deal with unexpected hurdles and new demands. You can exhibit readiness in the face of new things – also things you have not yourself chosen.

At other times, you are hijacked. You act or speak differently from what you normally would do or say. Possibly, you feel you suddenly are amateurish, unprofessional, beside yourself, difficult to cooperate with, a bad leader, an undesirable colleague, incapable of managing changes, unreliable, or, wide of your mark. Perhaps you have not discovered it yourself (since in this state of mind your consciousness is low), but perhaps your workmates might have realized it.

If you have a good feedback culture, perhaps they will tell you this, but in many cases, it is something only the others know, but they keep it to themselves. If you become aware of it, sometimes the realization strikes you so hard and make you feel terrible, but often you just talk in a little harsher tone than you intend, you act too hastily, you don't act at all, your tongue feels glued, you indulge in muddled talk – or other unintended behavior, that invades your better self. In the worst cases, you can feel regret, perhaps you feel sorry afterwards or simply angry with yourself. In the worst cases, you often become aware of it only afterwards. It came creeping without your discovering it. You have been hijacked.

"Can you recognize the pattern?" Caroline says at end.

"I can recognize it well," Marie says.

"Of course," Caroline says and straightens up her large spectacles again. "When you are in a ready state, you are distinctly better at collaborating with others, to function as a leader and to obey a leader. You are also notably better to tackle unknown circumstances and new developments you have not yourself chosen, and selfish leadership. When your brain is in a hijacked state, it becomes more difficult to be cooperative, to be a leader and to follow a leader – and to respond to a selfish leadership. You become limited in your thinking and your manner of action. However, by increasing your awareness you can practice staying in a ready state and avoid falling into a hijacked state. I can assist you with that. It can only have a good effect, not only on yourself but also for all others around you. Whether you are in a ready state, or a hijacked state can decide, whether there is a bridge between the kind of behavior you want to achieve and the kind of behavior you do in fact exhibit. When you are in a ready state, you can more easily *yourself choose, how you act and when.* When storm winds blow, you can with a hijacked brain react in a manner you regret, when the still returns – and first a while later you can think clearly again. Suddenly you can see the matter in several different ways, and you regret you were so aggressive, non-receptive or adamant – all according to your situation. This is a typical situation, in which your brain has been hijacked, and then you can think clearly again, first when your brain is in a ready state again.

The most provoking aspect of a hijacked mental state is that it often escapes your awareness, and you do not always manage to register, that you have been in a hijacked mental state. For it takes less than many people think to make your brain hijacked," Caroline says.

Marie can notice how engaged she is now. "Yes, because as I remember, the amygdala activates our fight-freeze-flight-response and it gives rise to a hijacked mental state, because I my body and brain cannot distinguish between whether I am in a fight or whether I am in an unreasonable situation at my workplace. For example, with Martin," Marie says, as if in a moment of enlightenment.

"Exactly," Caroline says visibly content.

Caroline begins writing on the whiteboard to describe in detail the triggers, which in reality are more or less the same. It can be situations like:

- Lack of confidence about your status in the group, or whether you have support from the others.
- Reacts on change, if you have a strong need for security or a knowledge of the future.
- Limitations, becomes provoked if you have a dire need of autonomy.
- You can react also when your status and position are challenged.
- Disagreement as to what is fair. Although justice is a universal standard, justice is often tinged with subjective interpretations, and it depends on the situation itself.

"Really, what happens in the now is not determination entirely on its own what you are feeling in that moment. It is an experience from the past that your brain is using to make sense of what you are experiencing now. Your brain has most likely interpreted the situation instantly – or before you arrive. Even though it feels like you are being triggered by an external event, it is really your brain reliving a past experience that somehow has some similarities. Those similarities can be subtle, but we can find the past experiences that formed your brain.

In practice, complex situations deserve consideration from many viewpoints. You can talk about persons who are difficult to work with, about a difficult conversation, bullying, a bad work environment, etc. However, in the final analysis, most people try to do the best they can, with what they have, and manage the situations they are in as well as they can. Problems with leadership and cooperation blossom up and propagate when persons come into a hijacked mental state. We can of course be in total disagreement yet arrive at a solution by talking, provided both sides are in a state of readiness. Being in a hijacked mental state can have an overpowering effect. Neurochemically the same processes occur in your brain and body when you are in a hijacked state as when you are in a state of stress, giving out physical, moody, emotional, and behavioral signals. If you train your awareness to detect the signals your body sends out, you can learn how to avoid in some cases coming into a hijacked mental state. When you enter a hijacked state, the following things occur in your body:

1. The amygdala informs the hypophyses that danger
    is looming.

2. Then it begins to produce the stress hormones adrenaline, noradrenaline, and cortisol.

3. They activate the sympathetic nerve system.

4ᵗʰ Tool: Switch nerve systems

Also, Caroline shows Maria a drawing as seen beneath, and she explains about the typical reactions that take place in the body, when you enter a hijacked mental state, and the sympathetic nervous system is dominant.

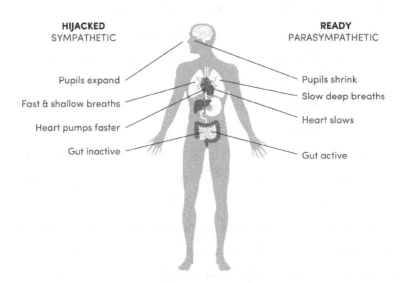

HIJACKED
SYMPATHETIC

READY
PARASYMPATHETIC

Pupils expand

Fast & shallow breaths

Heart pumps faster

Gut inactive

Pupils shrink

Slow deep breaths

Heart slows

Gut active

Fig. 3: The body's reactions when ready and when hijacked©, Campbell (2023).

HIJACKED

The sympathetic nervous system is active, And you use much personal energy. This means that you can experience:

- Tunnel vision
- Superficial breathing
- Fast pulse
- Digestion stops

READY

The parasympathetic nervous system can be active, And you can restitute yourself and load up. When you're ready you will experience that:

- The pupils become dilated, since when an animal must flee or fight, it needs to have tunnel vision.
- Your heartbeat increases to pump blood out to your arms and legs, so you can run faster.
- This is one of the reasons why resources are borrowed from your frontal lobes and your digestive tract.
- There is greater need for blood and oxygen to the arms and legs, when you need to run, than for empathy and absorbing nutrients in the bowels.

Mental states like having to focus, feeling stress and fear can activate the sympathetic nervous system. The sympathetic nervous system is activated when the brain thinks that a struggle for survival is imminent, even though you may be just sitting doing some important last-minute work or are outdoors jogging or you are arriving late for an appointment. Your sympathetic nervous system can be active even when you sleep, but your sleep will not be good. To sleep you need to be in a calm state, so that your parasympathetic system is activated.

Your parasympathetic nervous system can be dominant only when your sympathetic nervous system is calm. It needs a little time for your body chemistry to adjust, after the "danger" has passed. The transition from the sympathetic nervous system growing calm to the parasympathetic nervous system becoming active can need anything between a couple of minutes to several hours.

However, there is one thing that can speed the transition up. Slow, deep breathing. Breathing is the only one of the vital functions you have mastery over. You cannot control your heartbeat, but you can control your breathing. When you practice slow, deep breathing, your body sends signals to amygdala that there is no danger present. Consequently, it stops sending signals to the hypophysis to produce adrenaline and cortisol.

"Therefore, it is a good idea to "get a breath of air," when you feel a conflict is emerging, so you can get your parasympathetic nervous system active again, and then you will most likely see in a broader light what you earlier saw with tunnel vision."

"That makes sense. I would like to start learning how to meditate," Marie says.

"Yes, let's get you started as soon as it makes sense in the process," Caroline says.

Marie gives a nod. "Oh, how I have pressed myself hard. Or on second thoughts, how has Martin pressured me hard," Marie says thoughtfully.

"I believe we must spend our next meeting delving deeper into the matter, and then we can finalize with how to meditate. What do you want to take with you from today's session?

Marie thinks for a while, she looks at her notes and then she replies: "I am a bit overwhelmed by the fact that I have put myself under such hard pressure and have been allowing martin to do it too. I have to make some changes."

FOUR

Looking back

How are you today? Caroline looks a Marie.

"I am O.K. today. I am motivated to find out how it came this far. How could I let myself down this way?"

6th Tool: Stress timeline

"Let us look at when it all started. I call this exercise Stress Timeline, Caroline explains, and takes out a sheet of paper and a pen. "Please tell me when you first began to feel pressured, so we can show it on the timeline we have drawn here on the paper."

Caroline smiles and looks at Marie encouragingly, as she holds her pen, ready to write.

"Hmm, it must have been half a year ago," Marie says.

Caroline draws a line. "In March?" she asks.

"Yes," Marie answers with confidence.

Caroline writes March beside the line. "What happened then?"

"We had a big reorganizing, and Martin fired one of our other product leaders, Abigail, and I took over her work tasks. Not her department or title, only her work tasks. I really became strained with duties as I also had to substitute as leader for her employees. Unofficially, that is. The worst of the matter was, I felt that Abigail was unbelievably good at her job, but she took Martin by the horns quite often. They were not seldom at loggerheads at our monthly meetings. She refused to accept his scathing remarks," Marie says thoughtfully.

"What happened then?" Caroline asks.

"I really became piled up with work, but when I really think back, it happened before that. In fact, it was at our annual summit meeting, which we have each summer, for the product leaders alone, that the whole of my problems started. That was the first time Abigail had a real confrontation with Martin, and the result was a thoroughly bad atmosphere among us product leaders. Because some of us took side with Abigail and others took side with Martin, and I could not really choose a side on which to be. I am not good at giggling behind people's backs, and I sympathized with Abigail, whom Martin victimized during the rest of that summit, and it really was obnoxious. Neither was it reasonable. That was the first time I experienced how unpleasant he can be. I had heard rumors but never experienced him like this," Marie says emotionally stirred.

"And what happened?" In the meantime, Caroline keeps making sketches at full blast on the timeline.

"Come to think of it, a year and a half before that I was at one of my first meetings for product leaders, and I was full of enthusiasm, and might have even been a little irritating, but I had a whole lot of ideas. Martin was sitting at the far end of the long meeting table, and after I had had the word a couple of times, I heard him say, 'Is there anyone who can hear what she is saying? Oh, never mind, she always says a lot of overenthusiastic crap.' I was so shocked. I felt quite shaken after that meeting. I think that was when it started," Marie says, looking at Caroline's timeline.

"All right. We put a mark there. What happened afterwards?" Caroline asks and gives Marie a smile.

"That remark really hurt; it just came out of the blue. I had never seen him like that before, and it was in fact he that came and asked if I would like to be product leader on Blue Wonder, which is X-Corp's largest and most important area of activity, so I think that he must have judged me to be competent in my work.

"Now, as I think about the matter, it began when they promoted me. That means, it was the summer of two years ago. After we had attended my first summit meeting for product leaders, Martin said to me, after a good meeting and after wishing us a good flight home, and after he had just praised me – just after we placed our hand luggage over our seats, he looked at me suddenly and said: 'It must be hard for you to be feeling so happy about your promotion since the whole matter depends on whether I still think it's a good idea. I can fire you with a snap of my fingers if I want to." He took his satchel and went out of the airplane. I said nothing for many minutes in the car on my way home, after David and the children came and fetched me. I felt completely in a state of shock. I began to doubt whether he had said that. Can you follow?" Marie looks at Caroline directly. Caroline nods.

"What happened then? Shall we go farther back in time?" Caroline looks at Marie with warmth.

Marie thinks and says: "No, because I was under Abigail earlier and everything improved and got better. She cheered me on. She was such a good mentor for me. I learned so much from her," Marie stops talking and smiles quietly.

"Good, so we arrive at a conclusion that two years ago, Marie, you began to move downwards on your stress ladder and move away from yourself," Caroline says and looks at the paper.

Marie too looks at the paper and appears quite shocked. "Two years, that's a long time."

"Marie," Caroline says in a serious voice. "Two years with stress is a long time for your nervous system and your brain. Most people would have given up by now. It is very important that you get some peace and quiet now."

"Fortunately, I have not reached that stage," Marie says.

"No one who is really under stress wants peace and quiet. It is quite normal when you feel stress to try to manage with the situation at hand. The stress response is a survival technique that nature has created to help you win over your circumstances."

"I believe I have omitted to tell you, that David, the children and I are going off on vacation next week. We are going sailing for a week. I would feel very disappointed if I had to cancel our trip," Marie says.

"That I can understand. Perhaps there is no need for that. I am here to help you. If you can get a good rest, perhaps it can be the best solution, since you are so much at ease in the company of David and the children. The situation would be different if your family environment were more demanding. However, the children are fairly grown up and David shows great empathy. Your personal life is filled with good fortune. I suggest the following:

1. You go off on a vacation next week.
2. You begin this evening practicing the breathing exercise, I will teach you. Do it both morning and evening.
3. We inform Susanne in writing that you would like to take your vacation next week and we feel that will improve your situation, taking into account the circumstances leading up to that time off work.
4. When you return, you must have a lighter workload for at least two weeks more. Afterwards, we can judge your condition."

"Two weeks more is a long time," Marie says.

"What if I had said six?" Caroline replies with firmness, but in a friendly tone. "I would say so in many other cases, where the nervous system is more worn out. However, you are relatively young and otherwise in good health. You have a long working life ahead of you. The last time I was in my bank and talked about my pension, they calculated with my continued working life up to the age of 72 years. I myself plan to continue even longer than that. I love my work. You too must keep on for many years, and you can achieve this only if you take good care of yourself. What you can achieve as a leader does not become obsolescent. There will without doubt be need of you. I know it is hard to be idle, when you are used to being highly productive. So, let us finish by discussing what you can do and let's practice a meditation. It is soon time for me to meet Martin. Usually we involve the leader immediately above you in a three parts conversation. However, the way you are now, I think it is best I have a meeting with him alone and ask him about his view on the situation," Caroline says and straightens her large glasses.

"Yes," Marie says and lowers her eyes. "I am not ready now at any rate."

"I fully agree," Caroline says.

"Best of luck," Marie says a little drily. "And be well prepared. He is quick off the mark, well formulated and probably the most intelligent person I have ever worked with. He is extremely clever and very charismatic. Truly charismatic," Marie says with great emphasis on the word "charismatic."

"Okay," Caroline says and smiles. "Good to know. Let us make a list of things you can do now. What gives you restfulness?"

"Going for a walk with the dog, hard exercise with weights and doing crochet." Marie quickly replies.

"Going for a walk is really good. So is doing crochet. Hard exercise produces adrenalin, which helps you to stay in form, but see if you can do something else that is a little softer, not to release stress hormones," Caroline answers. "Is there anything else?"

"I also like reading."

"Good – do it," Caroline answered and smiles.

"And the company of my friends and colleagues.". She smiles at the thought.

"If, there is someone who expends your energy, so keep away from that person right now. You can still include them in your life. However, choose the few who can enjoy your company for your sake – without your being something or giving something to them.

FIVE

A selfish boss

Caroline arranges a meeting with Martin a couple of weeks later. Not that it was difficult for Caroline to book it with him, but it was not easy either. He would like very much to help Marie, as he repeatedly and clearly said many times, as he would like to participate in Marie's recuperation, so she can become well again. Of course. However, as to whether he has time to do so, that is an entirely different matter. They find a time however a couple of weeks later, especially after Caroline emphasizes that she herself will come out to meet him, and this would save some time for him.

"Hi," Caroline says in surprise, when she arrives at X-Corp and has just entered the reception. "How long have you stood here?" Caroline asks.

"A couple of minutes. I really hate when people arrive late. It is so lacking in respect for other people's time. Yes, you can hear this is one of my favorites," Martin says with a light in his eyes.

Caroline smiles. "Then it's a good thing, I always arrive in good time."

"We can meet in there," Martin says and indicates with a gesture with his head the door at the opposite end of the office area.

"Perfect," Caroline says and begins to walk towards the door. Caroline notices that Martin keeps his gaze straight in front of him as he walks through the open office landscape towards the meeting room. Four employees sit there working with their computers and they all raise their heads to give a greeting, which she knows is the custom at the office, but Martin ignores them. He quickly takes a seat, when they go inside the meeting room, takes out a notebook and a pen, which he lays on the table in an orderly way.

"I am ready. What is it you especially want to talk about on the subject of Marie? I have unfortunately only half an hour, after which I have to attend another meeting," Martin says and smiles again at Caroline with a quick, friendly smile.

"Then we must get as much done as possible in the time," says Caroline. "Let us first define the purpose of this meeting: We are here because Marie seems on the verge of a breakdown. In order to help you as best I can, I would like to hear your view since you are her next superior in line. I understand there had been a meeting, at which Marie broke down, shortly before she consulted me. You were present at the meeting. I would like to hear from you what you witnessed there and what you otherwise know about Marie? It is my experience that there are always several viewpoints from which to look at the same matter. In this matter, we are not trying to find right or wrong. We are trying to find solutions applicable in your case. There is always an opportunity to develop further when such a situation crops up. This applies to both of you. If you choose to consider the situation as an opportunity for development, your attitude can provide a means of ingress to the next tier of your development. But the question is whether you have the inclination to look at the matter from this viewpoint. We have only half an hour today, so we must limit our ambitions correspondingly. To hear your views on the matter would be a realistic target for today. You are welcome to come to my office for a talk, if you feel inclined to hear more about the avenue to your next stage, if you want to give it a go," Caroline says with a self-assured and teasing lilt in her voice.

Martin sits in the grip of surprise. He is not used to having such a challenge tossed at him – and this one could perhaps be entertaining, he thought. He immediately begins to tell about his childhood, the place where he grew up with his parents who were both psychologists. His childhood was difficult, but he met his wife already when he attended college, and they have stayed together as a couple ever since then. No children, only a dog. He interrupts himself:

"Yes, the pressure from work is great at X-Corp, so it's a matter of giving a higher priority to what is most important. However, I will give Marie a higher priority, but I see a lot of challenges facing her," Martin answers. "Alfred left the matter in my hands. She is the product manager for Blue Wonder, and good product managers like her are not to be found everywhere," Martin concludes by saying, returning Caroline's friendly expression.

"That I understand. But if you only have half an hour, should we not go directly into the heart of the matter?" Caroline asks.

"Yes," Martin says and leans back in the chair.

"Perfect. I would like to begin with the point you yourself have brought forward. What challenges do you see Marie has to meet?" Caroline asks with interest, the while looking at Martin with friendly attention.

Martin looks calmly at Caroline and does not answer a short while. Caroline lets him think all he can and sits still in her chair.

"Marie still has much to learn. She is relatively new in her job. Often, she behaves as if she is still an employee without the responsibilities of a leader. It is as if she has not fully understood how to practice true *leadership*. After the two years she has functioned in her job, I feel in my capacity as her superior that I can expect a greater productivity from her." Martin lets his gaze travel round the room and looks at Caroline again. "She needs to learn to let things fall by the wayside and not stop to pick them up. She has a penchant for lingering too long on details, analyzing them repeatedly. Like a true top-of-the-class schoolgirl, when results are not just what she expected, I sometimes think. The last bit is just my own opinion," Martin ends by saying, still sitting in a reclining position.

"You could also attribute it to her conscientiousness and tenacity?" Caroline asks showing interest.

"Yes, that can be another name for it, well said, and those are also good qualities," Martin gives a smile, "but we are talking about a high performance workplace, where every minute counts. Sometimes it can be difficult to motivate the employees to cope with the work. We need people of the right caliber who can withstand the strain of the work. Alfred and I need to acknowledge this fact," Martin says still reclining in his chair.

"Do you not recognize these qualities in Marie?" Caroline asks, straightening her glasses for the first time during the meeting.

"Yes, certainly. If only Marie could stop thinking too deeply and ignore the spilled milk and just carry on regardless. Make her employees get a move on. Then she would move up to become a shining star," Martin says. "But is she able to do that? What do you think?" Martin asks. Martin clasps his hands behind his neck and leans farther back in the chair, as he makes this last remark.

"I think Marie can develop to become whatever she wants to be," Caroline says, "the only question is whether it will be in keeping with the suitable leadership learning which she needs. However, we can question her on the matter. I have received the task of getting Marie ship-shape again, and we are fully engaged in this process. Let us keep this in mind," Caroline says as a final remark.

"I too aspire to become a truly brilliant leader, who can bring out the best in my subordinates and make them become stars. I believe that if they shall have success in X-Corp, some pressurizing is necessary. This rule applies too to Marie's associates, even though it is Marie, who must do the choosing. She does not accomplish this, and to avoid the whole organization ending up in your hands, yes, sorry, Caroline, I hope you understand what I mean, I have to take over the matter myself." Martin sends Caroline a big, charming smile. He takes a large mouthful of coffee. They are silent again in the room.

"I know she feels as if she is between the devil and the deep blue sea. I am not stupid. When she tries to keep her employees from having to work at weekends and from unnecessary, in Marie's opinion, hard deadlines, she does not exert enough pressure on them and thinks much too much about their comfort than about herself and her own career. She is the product leader, and I am her boss. Together with her team, she has to deliver a product. This is a matter of fact. They can just as well learn this immediately. Yes, I regret having to say this, Caroline, but this is the plain truth, and Marie needs to realize this. I am sure she can achieve this. She just needs to learn…yes, avoid being so over-engrossed. With her subordinates, and with her analyses of each and everything. Let things go. Quicker completion of task and fewer thoughts – and especially feelings." Martin looks at Caroline inquisitively.

Caroline gives a nod. "I need to understand you clearly, you are saying, that that's the main reason why Marie is where she is today – she wears herself down, because she uses her energy wrong?" Caroline straightens her glasses a good deal.

"Yes, when you say it like that, I agree. She must learn to say "never mind that" and maintain her focus on the ball," Martin says and folds his hands again behind his neck.

"The ball?" Caroline asks.

"Yes, the ball. To direct the ball into the goal, to execute, to make her subordinates reflect and sense less, and just do the work," Martin says and looks inquisitively at the coffee cup and again at Caroline, "Yes, I'm sorry but that is the lay of the land."

"Sorry isn't necessary. It's important that you tell me your point of view," Caroline says, raising her hand to her chin.

The conversation comes to an end soon after, and Martin says he's sorry he doesn't have more time. He explains he has now gotten extra duties to do, among other things, because Marie is on sick leave, but he would of course like to be of help.

Right after leaving Caroline calls Susanne. Susanne picks up the telephone at once.

"I am excited to hear how it went," Susanne says after talking a little about the weather.

"You know I can't go into the details, but I feel I am beginning to understand the processes which Martin perhaps sets in action in his subordinates," Caroline says. Caroline takes a breath as if about to say something, but Susanne interrupts her.

"He is hard, perhaps, but he is also exceptionally competent. Many of the employees think he is fantastic because they learn so much from him. He is so full of drive. Many feel it is exciting to work under him. He serves as an inspiration for them as well," Susanne ends by saying.

"I understand that very well," Caroline says, "but we must also acknowledge that many employees struggle with themselves under his leadership," Caroline says in a friendly manner.

"I know that, Caroline. I will talk with him about that, when an opportunity arises, and I know, and you must know too, that it worries me that Martin does not consider it much of a problem, that his subordinates in fact become stressed under his leadership. In addition, it does not reduce the problem that Alfred does not hold Martin responsible. Alfred does not *believe* in stress as a concept. He makes his priorities in a different way, to be honest, not affecting the popularity he enjoys among his subordinates. He condones Martin's conduct, since he thinks Martin is an indispensable person. He often says to me when I delve deeper, that he does not know, how we would manage without Martin. He is the company's figurehead," Susanne says, a trifle apologetically.

"I know," Caroline says, and before she could say more, Susanne says.

"I got Martin to talk to you today. That is a step forward. It shows that he perhaps he is in the process of changing his ways. That's how I look at it," Susanne says with a little more energy.

"Unfortunately, it was only half an hour," Caroline says, "he did not have more time."

"Just think as to how many times he stayed away when we asked him to come. That I consider as a positive sign, absolutely."

SIX

Inner life

David and the children have gone off to play baseball. It is Saturday and it is quiet now in the apartment. It feels ambivalent for Marie to say no to things and give her own self higher priority. In a way, it feels nice to be alone at last, but on the other hand, it feels hard to stand and wave goodbye to them from the window as they make their way out into the world outside. David and the children on their way to have fun. However, she is not; this quiet time is good for her.

Her work right now is to get into better shape, which is what Caroline always says with a twinkle in her eyes. Marie both misses her work, which filled so great a role and at the same time, she misses it not at all. It gives her a pain in the stomach to think about her work right now, so Caroline has said she must refrain from doing so. When we think about the things that make us feel stressed, our bodies react just as if we are in the same situations. Therefore, must Marie, in trying to regain a better condition, try instead to think about something that makes her feel happy. There is an implicit balance, since we should not behave in a *Happy Go Lucky* manner when everything around us is falling in shambles, but when Marie is at home and away from her work, she should try to create glad feelings inside herself by doing nice, pleasant tasks – and she must relax to let her nervous system recuperate. It is also in order to feel bad and at a loss. However, all the depressive thoughts, when she attempts to assess the situation and find a solution she should store up for the sessions with Caroline, to avoid making her mental gramophone start playing and getting stuck in a groove – and draining her energy away.

Inner and outer energy are the most valuable assets Marie can have right now. Her present objective is to restore her level of energy. This she can do in many ways, and often many avenues of approach are needed, for example, sleep, fresh air, leisurely strolls, light exercise for persons in good condition (this is not suitable for Marie right now), nourishing food, laughter, rest and music – the things that make her feel at ease, without her needing to show good results. Marie enjoys gardening, so she works in the community garden a couple of hours at weekends. When she goes out in the garden and gets dirt on her hands, she feels relaxed and gets into contact with her inner self.

Marie has good contact with the world inside her. She grew up as a child in a religious family, so she is used to saying prayers, and this is to her advantage now that she needs to keep in contact with what is happening in her inner self. She has ignored it much too long a time. Contact with her inner person can work as a shortcut for her, Caroline says.

Everything that takes place within Marie's inner self is crucial for her inner strength, which she is in the process of restoring. She needs to discover what is right and what is wrong for her. When goes beyond her threshold, what contributes to her energy and what has meaning and importance. Not least, it is important for her to do a cleaning out in her inner life. There are thoughts and feelings, that are authentic and important, and there are thoughts and feelings resembling an echo from times past, obeying a *repeat* function with ever the same messages, that she should get a grip on herself and do a better job, that she carries everything on her shoulders, and if she relaxes, everything will collapse. Consequently, she has begun to practice awareness of the thoughts and feelings present in her inner self, so she can sort them out. Some people think many negative thoughts about others, but Marie is not like that. She has a very generous heart and always thinks the best possible about other people. If someone is unable to do a duty, she tries to understand and assist. One of her good qualities as a leader is her ability to help others to succeed and develop. However, she does not possess a similar acumen regarding her own abilities. She places extremely large demands on herself. Now she has begun listening to an inner voice that says she must get a grip on herself and just get on with the job. When she hears this inner voice, she can feel a tightening on the back of her arms, her stomach feels empty and she feels a lump in her throat. It is enough that you observe and register this feeling, Caroline says.

"You don't need to do more. When you become aware of these thoughts and feelings, which the autopilot in your brain delivers, it will be easier for you to pick and choose. It is not easy to steer something of which you are unaware. So just start by being aware."

It does not feel rewarding to look at some of the feelings. There are piles of ashamedness and the feeling of being insufficient connected with them. Marie knows what Caroline would say right now: "It is good going you feel awareness and are registering things. It means you are acting consciously. It is easier to work with something we are aware of than with something we are unaware of. However, put it aside and focus on restoring your energy – it must feel elating to restore the energy in your system."

Marie's feeling of awareness centers once more on the present moment. She senses the smooth floor under the soles of her feet.

Caroline meditates every day. This she confided to Marie. When Marie heard this, it wakened a call inside her. She could sense inside herself a desire to do likewise, so she declared her preparedness now – though Caroline does not normally introduce it at so early a stage. You should not embark on new demanding projects at the start of a project like the one we have now. However, Marie was adamant.

They now set up a plan that she should meditate for ten minutes every day, when she wakes up, while David and the children are still asleep. At weekends and when they are on holiday, she should meditate, immediately after brushing her teeth – as a part of her morning ritual.

There are many techniques for meditation, so Caroline led a guided meditation during the session using several different methods, so that Marie could choose the one that works best on her. Afterwards they made a recording to which Marie could listen. Now when she sits in the kitchen and meditates with her bare feet placed solidly on the smooth kitchen floor, she can hear Caroline's calm voice in her ear pods.

When Marie spontaneously feels like meditating now, it helps to remove her stress. Neurological tests have shown that meditation with deep breathing exercises transmits signals to the amygdala that there is no danger at hand. As a result, just simple breathing exercises are very effective at alleviating stress. Very many who receive counselling from Caroline learn at some stage to practice the art of meditation. It needs an effort for most people to get started. Especially if their instructor says, they must not have thoughts about anything. However, Caroline has much experience and Marie is in preparedness to sit down and turn her awareness inwards, with genuine curiosity as to what she can discover about herself, when she deliberately concentrates her attention on her breath, and increases the length of her exhalations – even when her thoughts keep arising, which is quite normal.

Our breathing is the only vital function, which we can control. Very few can control how fast the heart beats but we can all easily make our breathing slower and deeper and make our brain believe that the danger has passed. It stops producing the stress hormones that make Marie unwell now – perhaps that is how Marie finds vigor to react against selfish leadership more quickly than what is usual.

Meditation too can in the future contribute to the extra mental energy, which Marie needs to handle projects in the future at her workplace –most of all in confrontation with Martin. Again, in the future, she will need to win over each day without Caroline's help. She feels secure in the apartment here, now with the sound of Caroline's voice in her ears – she needs to be able to work with Martin again. However, she must not worry about that right now.

Things are not going easily today. Marie cannot rapidly achieve a state of calmness, which normally she can do, and she has sprung over several things already. Caroline says she should get started at roughly the same time every day, so she ought to begin soon. Time flies quickly here in the quiet apartment.

Marie gives a glance at a pair of soiled coffee cups and plates with spoons from their breakfast. It is typical of David and the children to forget to place them in the dishwasher. Should she put them in before beginning? No, time is flying. She must get started now. Instead, Marie looks through the window, thinking about her last sessions with Caroline. They have really discussed at great length, what it is that consumes and what replenishes Marie's energy. She has made a list of the pluses and the minuses. These show quite distinctly that she has a great deal of assets that can make her happy – and which give her energy. Her marriage with David is thriving and she lives in a closely-knit family bond with an intimate and frank relationship with David, the ever understanding, supportive and helpful David. She has beautiful children, with whom she enjoys good relations and despite the fact that she is introvert, her relationships with friends, colleagues and relatives mean a great deal. She is however not the type of person to be at the center of everything.

All that was on the list with pluses. Marie smiles. All too was on the list with minuses. She is too remiss at getting enough sleep, doing physical exercise, and eating a healthy diet. She knows very well what she has need of, and she has begun together with David and sometimes with Emma and Storm to prepare healthy meals. These are some of their best daily moments, when they stand around cooking and telling about the daily happenings.

They have as well found a couple of favorite vegetarian dishes. So, the minus sign here is changing over to a plus sign.

Caroline has also encouraged Marie to find a form of exercise, which perhaps does not compel socializing, since Marie is introvert and meets so many people every day at her workplace, losing energy in the process. A form of one-man exercise, perhaps, which she finds enjoyment in, enticing her to practice it regularly.

This has been a little more difficult. She has always gone for many walks with their dog, Jax, and now she can understand why she always has done so. It is just to savor the feeling of quietness and not be at the disposition of others. This has made her think that she should perhaps begin to go jogging with Jax. Marie's good friend, Barbara, jogs a lot. They have talked about Marie starting to run with her a little, and afterwards Marie can go off jogging by herself, when it is one of those days.

They begin next Saturday. After meditation, Marie drinks her second glass of water for the day. It is one of Caroline's pet topics that it is important for her to drink water.

Marie yawns. She did not have a good sleep last night. She strives very hard to get her sleep at nights now, since Caroline said that sleep is the most important element in her treatment now. She should sleep as long as she likes in order to improve her condition – even if it means sleeping during the daytime. For people suffering from severe stress, sound sleep is the best medicine. There is good sleep and there is bad sleep. Good sleep restores the nervous system. For this to happen, the parasympathetic nervous system must be in the ascendancy to allow proper restoration. When you engage in sporting activities, or have worries, are upset or stressed, this activates the sympathetic nervous system. Then you produce stress hormones and cannot truly replenish yourself. It is quite normal for people who work under pressure do not enjoy a good night's sleep. They simply do not replenish their energy reserves, which they need to do.

When Caroline and her co-workers using trackers of team energy, they nearly always find that the greatest energy loss takes place in connection with corporate politics, with activity that is unproductive and from lack of sleep. Sleep appears too on Marie's list with the minuses. That she slept too little mostly – and perhaps her sleep quality was bad as well, all of which is so crucial for a high energy level.

Lying in her bed, she thinks about Martin. What he has done and said to her and what he can contrive to do and tell her colleagues.

Marie has become truly observant about what it is that dissipates her energy. The main point on her list with minuses is Martin. It has become clear for her to see, that he is the one who transgresses her personal limits repeatedly. He asks her to do things conflicting with her sense of ethics and values. He asks her to behave like a person she is not. That she cannot do – at least not with integrity. She has tried for so long a time and now she is at home sitting in her apartment on a Saturday, and the only entry she has in her calendar is her morning meditation. Same time, same place, and same ten minutes.

Marie glances up at the clock in the kitchen, shuffles her feet a little, and now she can feel the kitchen floor and she closes her eyes and listens to Caroline's soothing voice guiding her to breathe in slowly and taking her to a nice place.

SEVEN

Trigger points

Marie is with Caroline again. They sit at the conference table. The afternoon sun shines in through the large windows.

"How are matters going?" Caroline asks, filling water into a glass for Marie, who has reached out for it.

"Things are not easy. I really do like my colleagues, in particular Mark and Uma. Everyone is nice to me. The project also is interesting. Anna is fantastic. What a calm way she has. But I feel stress. I feel a pressure welling up inside me. It comes from my own self."

"What is it about?" Caroline asks in a friendly voice.

"It is because I want to be of help to the others. It is difficult only to look on when my good colleagues come under stress. Uma is really in a bad shape – and she is so badly off that you can't talk to her about it. I doubt whether she knows what is happening to herself. It hurts me to be looking on from outside."

"I can easily understand that. You find it unbearable to see your colleagues on the brink of collapse. In principle, it should not be that way, and this creates a climate of stress that has made your mind prisoner, moving you over to the red area in the matrix. All persons experience having trigger points. There is some small difference as to which trigger points make us react most strongly, but generally they often fall under the same five categories," Caroline says and looks at Marie contentedly. "The question is only which ones you react on most – and which those around you that you work together with react on most. It relates to your past experiences and through which lences you see the world " Caroline continues.

Marie gives a nod. "It sounds very relevant for me, and I can feel this, just by you telling me about it," Marie says.

"I would like to explain it to you. It is more to convince you about what triggers you . There are five archetypical trigger points that shows the inter-personnel needs that our brain is guided by – fueled by fear or the expectation of a reward[2]. That is why you can act towards a reward or away from fear. We call them trigger points because, at one level or another all people pursue these five factors, some of which have a much greater importance for us than others, all depending on how we are." Caroline gets up and here is the elaboration of the five factors she writes on the white board:

7th Tool: Trigger points
Status – Your relative importance to others.
Caroline explains: "Status can reveal itself through titles and material well-being, like an expensive car. However, its expression can

---

2   The trigger points are from David Rock's work.

be much more subtle, in the form of having authority, an informal position of importance or losing face.

Certainty – your ability to foresee the future.

"Here certainty has relation to how foreseeable circumstances and future prospects are."

Autonomy - Your feeling of being master of situations.

"When you are autonomous, you are free to steer what happens to yourself."

Relations - How secure you feel in the company of others.

"This deals with how much at ease we feel with others is one of the primary elements we use to determine our bearings. It is here our feeling of being included in or excluded from a group belongs."

Fairness - How fair you view exchanges taking place between people.

"This trigger is about that justice bears the designation of a universal concept, but it is a subjective experience or a point of view that decides what is fair. It is a trigger point that can really deceive us, if we are not watchful and possess a high level of objectivity."

To summer up the five triggers are:

1. Status
2. Certainty
3. Autonomy
4. Relations
5. Fairness

The five triggers are present in the brain of all people unless you suffer from a brain injury or personality defect. No *normal* person can say that justice does not matter. It can have relation either to oneself or to others. Different values or opinions can form a basis for what justice is. The question however is how much we react on it.

These trigger points provide a good broad picture that you can use to reflect on and test yourself which things you react sharply or mildly on.

You can also use it to check cases where you suspect there are others who feel they have received bad treatment, or perhaps been unabashedly misjudged.

If you have undergone a good personal analysis, perhaps the test shows you have some trigger points that are dominant. For example, you may feel a strong compulsion to use checklists and taking no risks or a preference to use free expression and autonomy.

Your emotional make-up can also influence how you can lose your head. Your convictions and mental framework can affect the subconscious mechanisms in your thinking processes and the way your mind can get possessed. Traumas can also exert an effect. However, no two individuals are identical or react to a trauma in exactly the same manner.

"Hmm," Marie says. "It seems a little abstract for me right now. Are we going to begin from another?" Marie asks.

"Yes, but I have just a little more I will add before doing so. I would like to give you a few examples so it will seem less abstract to you hopefully. It does not always need a lot to set the brain in a state of alarm and it becomes possessed. If in advance, you are overwhelmed, burdened, tired, stressed, or vulnerable in some other way, sometimes no more is need than:

- You arrive late.
- You have to address a group.
- You must make decisions about innovative projects or about future strategies using as basis supposition and extrapolated, qualitative data instead of retrospective, quantitative data.
- You must take part in a difficult conversation or discussion.
- You must do something new, without knowing what it will lead to.
- You get interrupted.
- Several persons speak to you at the same time.
- You are ignored.
- Plans become altered.

It is seldom due to a single cause that a brain become hijacked. Often this is the result of a combination of factors. Really what is happening is not that you are getting triggered from the outside event. It is a a past event that your brain expects to repeat itself. Sp because there is something in the current situation that is similar, you get triggered.

"Does this make more sense now?" Caroline asks.

"Yes, it does," Marie answers and a furrow creases her brow. "It is very relevant for me right now. I can see that there are several factors that have been the reason why I broke down like I did," Marie says.

"When I look at the five triggers now and think about all the things we have talked about, I realize I have to some extent a tendency to take on too much responsibility." Marie says, biting her lip.

"Too much responsibility, so you say," Caroline says. "And how does it show up?"

"I become a little like a mother for my employees and take on their problems. Especially with regard to Martin, I mean. It slips my mind that they are adult individuals and should be able to stand on their own two feet." Marie answers. "I know that full well, but still, I cannot keep to myself. I believe it is because Martin crosses over my limits so much and I would like to protect them."

"So you take on responsibility for the whole department, where Martin is involved? Goodness, that sounds difficult," Caroline smiles.

"Yes in fact I do. I can see that now, that it is much too much. I believe they don't even know I do. Or thank me for it. I just do so," Marie says.

"Would it mean something to you, that they knew? Can they feel it, do you think?" Caroline asks.

"I never leave them to bear the burden when Martin is too hard on them, and I have tried to parry his attacks. However, I can see that I take too much responsibility on my own shoulders. As a leader, I have of course to protect my employees, but they must be able on their own to fend for themselves at their workplace. They are adult individuals," Marie says and shakes her head a little. Caroline says nothing. She can see that Marie has her eyes fastened on the five triggers on the whiteboard, and a lot is transpiring in her head.

"Perhaps I am a little too perfectionist," she says. "And I feel a yearning for justice. Matters must be conducted in a fair way, and my employees must feel themselves secure," Martin often brings a challenge, I feel. I shoulder the responsibility for my employees just a little too far, so I end up as the scapegoat. In some subtle kind of way."

"What do you think about that?" Caroline asks with interest.

"I especially feel a trigger point, when Martin goes behind my back and talks to my subordinates directly and I cannot follow and keep track of them –and I cannot be on the spot to look after the interests of my employees. It really upsets me, when he exploits them. That I pay the price is just part and parcel of my position as leader, I feel. I have myself climbed up there, but my subordinates have not done likewise. Yes, perhaps this sounds a little strange," Marie says.

"Could you tell me more details?" Caroline asks.

"I believe in fact, now we are sitting here and talking, that Martin really does what he does on purpose sometimes. He knows I don't like it. It is as if when he thinks things are going a little too nicely, he sights on one of my employees without my knowing. He did so when we two started this process. He had contacted my coordinator and questioned her about my fatal project, Blue Wonder in detail, asking her for information about it. She said to him she did not know about the details, and he should direct his questions to me. But he had persisted, and she had tried as she could. And whenever she showed hesitancy, he went to the attack.

"She had in fact said, she didn't know any details. She came to me in tears. I feel so helpless and in addition, a bad leader," Marie says and looks in protest at Caroline.

"But is it your responsibility, what Martin does?" Caroline asks.

"I have evidently thought so, I can see now, but of course I cannot bear responsibility for that. That is Martin's own responsibility.

I have chided myself for not expressing myself sufficiently clearly to Martin, since he keeps on doing the same, again and again. That my communication has been bad, and I fail as a leader. I so much yearn to do a good job. As the best of the best," Marie says.

"Okay – that's a good insight," Caroline says. Keep at it as I believe we are arriving at something important here."

EIGHT

Over-responsibility

"I have in fact thought a lot about what we discussed the last time – about assuming over-responsibility. I have gone some long walks the last few days with David, during which we talked about it. I thought about discussing that conversation with you today. It impressed me. I could suddenly see similarities with other things in my life – and perhaps understand why it's better also to be honest." Marie sighs and stares with a dreamy look in front of her. Caroline says nothing. She only smiles and waits.

"I told David about what we had discussed last, and it came out in that conversation that it's not only with Martin that I assume over-responsibility. It is with so many other things too. It was in fact a rather big wake-up call when we went here." Marie turns her head and looks at Caroline. "This is a wild ride I'm on with you. It has embodied so many other things." Caroline nods, smiles and listens.

"All our talk about my trigger points and over-responsibility awakened something inside of me, and when I walked here with David, it occurred to me how I grew to be this way."

"What can you feel in your body right now?" Caroline asks.

"Agitation."

"What else? Do you feel any physical sensations?"

"My upper arms feel tense."

"Anything else?"

"A hollow feeling in the top of my stomach."

"Try taking off your shoes, close your eyes, and place your feet on the floor, so you stand solidly on your feet. Breathe slowly. Feel the contact with the chair you are sitting on, feel the top of your head and feel your feet resting on the floor." There is quiet for a moment.

"Describe now the feeling of hollowness, Has it a form or a color?"

"Yes, it is a grey mass."

"Has it a material? Is it firm, soft, hard, smooth or what?"

"It is a little like smoke."

"What is your earliest recollection of the grey smoke? How old are you? You must not think too much, just say something, listen to your gut feeling – it comes from the limbic system in your brain, that can deal with several thousand impulses per second – and sees everything. Your forebrain, where your consciousness is situated, and your conscious thoughts have their abode can deal with only one or two impulses per second. So, there is reason in my request to you to answer with your gut feeling and not too much thought. What is your earliest recollection? How old are you?"

"I think I am about ten years old. I cannot quite remember, but at any rate, I am standing outside the door of my parents' bedroom.

"Are you alone, or are you together with someone?" Caroline asks.

"I am alone at home with my mother and my two younger siblings. My father was not often at home, so we children were very much under my mother's supervision, which unfortunately she found a difficult challenge. She was not much of a mother for us. The door is closed, and I know for some reason or other, it will remain closed a long time yet. I must have had this experience many times before, since I know of this fact, as I am not very old. However, I can remember this happening. Because I know unfortunately too what takes place on the other side at the height of a child. My mother called it 'taking a rest', but the truth is that she is lying under the influence of pills and alcohol. For many years, I believed parents just were like that, that they were all like that, as we never talked with anyone about my mother's 'rest', which she enjoyed in plenty and lasted for many hours, sometimes for days. My father ignored them also if he was home."

"How does it feel for Marie 10 years old?" Caroline asks quietly.

"Outwardly, my family had a reputation as decent and respectable people. My father worked in a bank and my mother was a housewife who works at home, so we have never really lacked money. As well, we lived in one of the larger houses on the street. We have never spoken about these things. My parents are still married. They keep their façade intact – also with regard to my siblings and myself. Now it is for the first time that I realize how very badly it functions in reality. However, when you do not talk about things, I can sometimes feel doubt as to whether I have remembered correctly. Whether I dramatize the whole thing a little too much. I know now, and I do not think I knew it then, that my mother was in the condition she was in, because my father was unfaithful to her. I did not understand that at the time. As an adult, I know now, but I can remember when he came home with presents and flowers to her, she forgot his unfaithfulness and on the face of it forgave him – and they lived happily together for a while. Or rather as happily as they could manage. Then my mother suddenly began taking the one rest after the other. Today my father is so old, that I do not think he still has need for those things. They seem to have found each other again in their retired life by playing golf and bridge with their friends. They seem to be living in more harmony now. My mother is a sensitive person, but it seems my father is devoting more time to her now – and this helps her. Perhaps now she is receiving the attention she always has wanted from him."

"Where is ten-year-old Marie?"

"I am standing outside my parents' bedroom door. I rap on the door and call out my mother's name and get no answer. Perhaps I recall this incident because I felt we were now back there again, and I would need to cancel my date with my best friend, Sofia, because I now had to look quickly and see if we had food, cook dinner, help my two younger siblings with their lessons, and give them a bath before bedtime."

"What does ten-year-old Marie need right now?"

"For my mother to wake up and open the door, give me a hug and say everything is fine, and we have to prepare our evening meal together," Marie answers moved.

"Imagine it happening. Look at their faces. Feel your mother's hug," Caroline says with warmth.

A long quiet pause follows. Then Caroline slowly guides Marie back.

"How was it?" Caroline asks frankly.

"It makes sense," Marie says quietly and rubs her face with both hands.

"How do you feel in your stomach now?" Caroline asks.

"It feels empty – the grey smoke has left," Marie says surprised.

"How do your arms feel?"

"I don't feel anything in my arms now. I feel relaxed. How remarkable this is. It makes sense. I have a very good relationship with my younger brothers and sisters today and they often ring to me if they have a problem. I have always played this role. I am the eldest. I have never felt this to be unusual – before now. I have spent my younger days looking after them, taking on much too great a responsibility. I have also used a lot of energy covering up the events that truly transpired, so no one should know about it. I still keep leaving trails in my life. This time it is Martin who provides me with a provocation. I expend so much energy trying to make matters appear shipshape and smoothing things out when conflicts are in the air or embarrassing situations arise. Does all this sound crazy?"

"Not at all," Caroline says. "I had an inkling there was some kind of provocative circumstance that explains your large need to assume responsibility. Too much responsibility on your shoulders not intended for you to bear. We cannot remove the anguish you have stored inside you from your childhood, but we can find a redemption.

Then you can store it somewhere else, where it won't bully you all the time."

"Oh, I really do hope we have solved that now. I can see now, how these experiences affect me – even now as an adult. I have not at all observed or believed there was a connection. They happened so long ago," Marie says.

"They hang together as one whole. Those past experiences make you feel especially triggered, when you see other people get hurt. It is not like other humans do not feel when others get hurt, but to you, it is like reliving the nightmare that you lived, when you were ten years old. When you feel redeemed from the pain you have carried all your adult life, the pain does not vanish, but it becomes less sharp, and it loosens its grasp on you. It will lose some of its power to trigger you. When we supposedly forget about our pain and carry it about unconsciously, it becomes easier for the pain to decide our behavior and fashion our personality. However, we humans are not static beings. We can form new neural connections in our brains our whole life. We can change ourselves our whole life. You can too. Look at it, as if you are a computer. You have a hard drive, which is a steering system, and what you learn, these are new apps. What we just redeemed corresponds to a *bug* in your steering system."

Caroline reaches to an end. It is time to round off the day.

NINE

Extrovert work life

Two weeks have passed since the last session. Marie is sitting, pale and perspiring, in Caroline's meeting room. Martin has summoned Marie to an hour-long face-to-face meeting. It is time for *The Annual Performance Review*. Marie is taking a break. Caroline can almost feel how she is shuddering.

"Martin is a very eloquent and quick-acting leader, who enjoys and derives nourishment from the company of others, whereas you are introvert and your strength lies in your careful deliberation. Do you agree?" Caroline asks and looks at Marie inquisitively, while straightening her large spectacles.

"I agree completely. I have in fact not thought about the role it plays. I have had this analyzed through the tests I have taken in connection with job interviews, but these things have been verified rather than explained to me as to their implications," Marie answers and leans forwards more, placing the palms of both hands on the table.

"When you are introvert, you replenish yourself best in most cases in your own company. Typically, you think before you talk. Instead of thinking while you talk. In keeping with their nature, many introverts observe things more than extroverts do. However, they can just as in your case, have need for a little time to think and find the right answers and make them quickly. The rules that apply at a workplace direct themselves to extroverts mainly. Your listeners expect you to give a quick reply – otherwise it can seem you do not really know what you are discussing.

"However, a problem arises in that if we will be truly inclusive, then we must also be inclusive with regard to different personality types, but circumstances are not always conducive to this. However, with mindfulness of the fact that you yourself are introvert and what this means in your case, can you find it easier to navigate – and also easier to navigate with regard to Martin," Caroline says. "For example, I've noticed you have shifted your posture and are sitting almost in a power pose. I'll return to that a little later. Just remember the feeling you have in your body now," Caroline smiles a little secretively.

"Like now?" Marie says and leans forward more. "It feels in fact good – as if I am ready, as if I have control over the situation," Marie says and grins a little at herself.

"Remember this feeling. You can keep sitting there about two minutes, while I talk a little more about being introvert as compared with being extrovert," Caroline begins. "In our part of the world being extrovert is often the choice that is preferred and rewarded – and the world of business, wherein you are employed, is designed to suit extroverts. Just think how it is when you are off on strategy seminars or conferences, how fatiguing it is for you and other introvert participants not to have a moment at your own disposal, because there are so many social events, when there are no technical activities taking place. It can challenge introvert persons like yourself in other ways. Especially because I often see my introvert clients in my coaching lessons trying to 'get a hold on themselves', so they can become somewhat more extrovert. Some achieve this, but it takes great toll on their energy resources. As a leader, you must be able to give a quick answer. Most introverts function best when they can spend a little time thinking before, they give their answer. Sometimes the solution is to accept whom you are and utilize the qualities you have. Introverts can do just as much as extroverts can do. Most of us possess both introvert and extrovert qualities, but we always have an overriding amount of the one or the other. An extrovert like Martin flourishes best when he is in contact with others and finds it easy to join in small talk, whereas you, being introvert prefer to focus and concentrate on a single subject. This does not imply that you cannot engage in small talk, behave in the right way with other people or act with quickness. However, it needs more preparation on your part and it consumes your energy, and this you will need quiet and time to replenish. Martin, on the other hand, thinks quickly without needing much preparation and he derives energy from the company of others. That's where he tanks up." Caroline gets to her feet and begins writing on the white board.

"This might be a little squared to see people this way, and we can also argue that the world is not as black and white as this, but this perspective might be useful in your case right now"

According to Meyers Briggs, who did on of the first large personality test, the following characterizes an introvert person.

- You like to delve to great depths and must preferably not be disturbed in the meantime.
- You make unduly large preparations for your presentations and the like.
- You love to be alone at times and you relax best in your own company.
- You are not attracted to small talk and large gatherings.
- You think before you talk.
- You prefer to listen rather than talk.
- You do not like to be interrupted and therefore you seldom interrupt others.

The following characterizes an extrovert person:

- You derive energy from being together with other people.
- You relax best in the company of other people.
- You speak loudly and gesticulate with your arms at the same time.
- You talk before you think.
- You can most times give a quick reply.
- You work best in a group.
- You like multitasking.
- You can interrupt others without giving it a thought.

"You do not need to place a tick next to everything, but can you in a general way recognize your own character in one of these columns? Caroline asks.

"Oh, how apparent it is, when you tabulate it in that form. Where I stand and where too Martin stands. We are diametrical opposites with regard to so many things. "It's quite explainable then, why I keep getting conflicts with him," Marie says, letting her eyes roam over the white board. "It has suddenly become very clear to me, why I react in a certain way in certain situations – especially in cases where I derive energy from certain situations and lose energy in others. Now also, since I have the function of a leader, and I am together with so many people all the time. Also, when I have planned to spend some time before my computer and I need to go deeper into a problem, and my subordinates keep interrupting me all the time. I would like to be of help, but this drains me too. I was not like this before, when I was the project leader. During that period, I suffered fewer disturbances."

"It is important to know, what your natural tendency is – especially when you are obliged to perform another function than the one suited to the tendency you have. In order to keep a watchful eye on your energy. As you yourself have expressed in several connections, Martin talks more than he listens. He interrupts you often without noticing it – and he derives energy from activity and action, preferably in the company of others, and the others are often yourself. It drains Martin on the other hand when you try to make him concentrate on the same thing for a long time. You on the other hand are more pensive and do not indulge in small talk. You are attentive and on the lookout. You need "alone" time, and you run out of energy, if you have to be 'turned on' for too long an interval. However, Martin demands this of you – so does your job. You are good at concentrating for long periods without a string of interruptions like fetching coffee or looking at your telephone, if you get the time and give yourself the privilege. Do you ever work from home?" Caroline asks ending up.

"No, because then I don't feel I have control with what Martin does, and how my team is managing. However, I can see, now that we are talking about this, that it would be advantageous for me sometimes. Then I can replenish my energy reserves and get peace and quiet and a space for deeper thinking. I really miss that," Marie says with a sigh.

Caroline continues. "It is rather much a matter of learning to know your own energy economy. We will talk more about that after the next two sessions, when I will introduce you to the energy barometer. With a knowledge of this, combined with the other assets at your disposal, such as your tenacity, you are in a better position to achieve your goals than Martin, who is more susceptible to adverse reaction from his environment. Though the outside world can seem more easily within the reach of extroverts, there are nowadays developments under way that suggest a change that will benefit the introverts. There is more focus on the values an organization has, which eminently include the work climate. That is attracting much more focus now," Caroline says.

"I sit thinking about my annual performance review, which I soon must present together with Martin. It fills me with anxiety. Can some of what we have talked about now be useful in this regard?" Marie asks, looking up at the whiteboard again. "It's just a thought."

"It can indeed," Caroline answers. "That is why we talk about it now. If you look up at the whiteboard, you will need less talking, deep thought and reflection. It contrasts with Martin's planned meeting with duration one hour, in which he will talk a lot, hurry extremely quickly through the whole curriculum and try to reach to a hurried conclusion. I think you should try to establish that the meeting be held in two halves, each lasting thirty minutes and with a day in between. In the first half, he will talk, and you will listen. Before you must give answers, you have twenty-four hours for reflection and preparation. In this way you can keep up with the pace, can you follow me?"

8th Tool: Power poses

Marie rises to her feet and walks over to the white board. "I get in fact an uneasy sensation in my body at the thought of this meeting, but when you make these suggestions, they relieve the situation. A great deal, but not wholly. Is there something else we can do?" Marie asks and turns towards Caroline, who remains seated.

"Yes, can you remember when you leaned forward at the start of our conversation and rested the palms of your hands on the table? It was almost a power pose. Are you familiar with power poses?" Caroline asks. She raises her feet so they hang over the edge of the table and folds her hands behind her neck.

"Is that what you're doing now? Marie asks grinning. "Should that help?"

"Yes, that's what it is. This one is a little difficult to practice at your workplace in an open office landscape, but there are several power poses. Social psychologist and bestselling author, Dr. Amy Cuddy by name, has scientifically proved that holding power poses for two minutes makes your testosterone level rise and this makes you more intrepid and less fearful. Power Poses are naturally only a single tool from the toolbox but they function as a good supplement to all the other things we talk about," Caroline says, as she gets to her feet. "If you had risen, when you leaned over the table with the palms of your hands on the table, you had assumed a power pose. Another power pose is if you stand like Superman with your legs apart and with your hands placed on your waist." Caroline shows Marie how to do it. "Come and try yourself," Caroline says, beckoning with her hand.

Marie rises up and imitates Caroline a little awkwardly.

"It is not my intention you should do this in your office," Caroline says with a smile, still standing in the same posture, "but you can sneak into an empty meeting room or a toilet just before the meeting and stand in this posture and keep doing so for two minutes, so you affect your neuro-chemical balance."

Marie smiles.

"It gives a nice feeling in fact," she says, waving her arms a little.

"You can also keep standing, as you do with your legs," Caroline says, and so doing, she raises her arms up stretched slantwise, so she almost resembles a cross. "And stretch your arms slantwise, like I am doing." Marie imitates her.

"Can you feel it?" Caroline asks, still standing in the posture.

Marie nods. "Really nice. What a good help."

"Now you are ready for your annual performance review structured in two halves with one day in between," Caroline chuckles.

TEN

Healthy cooperation

A couple of months have passed, and Susanne has summoned Marie to a meeting, for which she has formulated a loose agenda of discussing Marie's job satisfaction. Susanne has brought her colleague Helena; it's always a good thing to have extra eyes and ears at this kind of meeting. Marie belongs to the inner circle of employees, and she knows that Alfred is a little worried about whether they might be losing her. It seems however that everything is progressing well once more, according to what Susanne and Helena have heard in various places. Now they intend to check out whether Marie too shares this opinion.

The meeting is well under way. They have dealt with all the informal topics and Susanne wants the meeting to center on the main agenda.

"We want really to hear in peace and quiet, how you are doing, Marie," Susanne asks and smiles benevolently at Marie. They do not know each other very well and it is mostly Caroline who has steered the conversations with Marie.

"Everything is okay," Marie says and returns her smile. "I really feel I have had a good process with Caroline. It has been of great help to me."

"Oh, we are so glad to hear that. I want to hear how things are going between you and Martin– and do you have your energy back?" Susanne continues questioning.

"I think I have begun to find a way to make things function. It is not so that I get out of bed every morning with energy. But I manage my tasks quietly and calmly, and I avoid the pitfalls," Marie says clearing her throat. "Martin's sharp edges," she says with distinctness.

"Martin, yes, that too is something I would like to talk with you about," Susanne says.

"I will never succeed in reconciling myself with his behavior, and this takes its toll, even though I make frequent use of Caroline's methods," Marie interrupts without letting Susanne finish speaking.

"Hmmm," Susanne says and looks inquisitively at Helena, who keeps her eyes fixed on her notebook and her pen."

"I hope the situation is not intolerable for you. In any case, we would like to offer our help, would we not, Helena?" Susanne says, trying again to get a response from Helena.

Helena turns her gaze upwards. She looks first at Susanne and then at Marie. Then at Susanne again. "Yes, of course, that is the reason why Susanne has convened the meeting, because Martin wants to make concessions on your behalf, Marie," Helena says, keeping her gaze fastened on Susanne.

"Precisely," Susanne says, visibly relieved. "In order to foster better cooperation between Martin and you and bury the hatchet, we have managed to make Martin agree to hold a meeting with both Caroline and you. We believe a three-party meeting will make it easier for Martin and you to patch up your differences and work together in the future. He has never done this before." Susanne clears her throat. Yes, it has developed in an unexpected way. However, we only want to know if you are game to having a meeting like this, if so then we will arrange it in Caroline's office."

"Caroline has told me about this already, and of course I am willing," Marie says with a swallow.

"Excellent," Susanne says, "We'll write it in the calendar."

A week later Martin and Marie take part in a meeting in Caroline's office. Caroline in her invitation to the three-party-meeting stressed unequivocally that she hoped the meeting would take place in a positive spirit. They should not talk about problems. They must not dig a ditch between them but instead they must build bridges founded on common values and similarities. Both Martin and Marie agreed to this.

A three-party-meeting is with coachee, direct manager, and coach: Coachee is sharing selected findings and objectives. Coach is observing and supporting. A three-party meeting can have a special objective as in this case, or it can be to share insights, aspirations of a development process and to get the direct managers input to the coaching process. With a three-party-meeting the coaching process is attached to the organizational reality and possibility of creating an alternate reality in the coaching process is minimized.

They are sitting at the meeting, which is well under way. They are engaged in small talk, but Caroline steers the discussion about what qualities they saw in each other at the start of their collegial activities. She asked them to do a single exercise together, in which they should write the names of things they have in common on a blackboard.

The things they write that they have in common are:

- That they both have a passionate interest in creating processes.
- That they both are born and raised in another country.
- That they both are married to one of their school mates.
- That they both own a dog they love to go for walks with.
- That they both want to attain the goals set for Blue Wonder before the deadline set.
- They both have an interest in quality.
- They are both ambitious.
- They both find pleasure in helping others develop themselves.

Martin and Marie step back a pace and look at the list of things they have in common, as it stands on the whiteboard. There is a calm in the room and a feeling of accomplishment.

"How does it feel to look at this list?" Caroline asks.

There is a pause. Marie is the first to answer. "It'svery nice to have called to mind all the things we have in common and many of the good thoughts, we talked more about at the start. It feels a little like coming back on the right course."

Martin gives Marie a slanting look, as if he just needs to get her approval – and then he begins talking. "It is fantastic. However,

I always say, Marie is so fantastic. If only she could learn to make mistakes, then she would become even more fantastic. Sometimes we need to drop things and let them fall on the floor, when we can see, they don't produce anything. *Fall fast forward.* In matters of this nature, Marie is far too nice."

Marie's shoulders shrug themselves closer to her throat, as if she is about to pack herself away. Then Caroline picks up the pencil and moves over to another white board in the room.

"Good work. You have quite a lot in common. A lot to work together on, and in many ways your personalities supplement each other really well. You have much in common, but you differ widely, and this provides an asset, when you have to solve complex problems together, to move a whole organization forward in difficult circumstances and to find new incentives. Research provides unequivocal results. Diversity in an administrative forum leads to finding better solutions and gives increased innovative skills. However, it exacts a requirement from you too. It can be more difficult to cooperate with someone who is not similar to yourself than with someone who thinks and acts in the same manner as you do. The demand is that you master the art of accepting that we differ." Caroline starts making a drawing all the while she still keeps on talking.

9th Tool: The 3 relationship circles

"Leadership and cooperation are concerned with reaching some targets in collaboration. A collaboration or corporation is a relationship. Here are depicted three different relationships. Where the distance separating the persons are not the same. Each circle represents a person. As a result, there are three relationships involving two persons in each. In principle, more than two persons can be involved, which gives more circles in each relationship. However, to make it easier to understand, we involve only two persons here – and right now, we are discussing only the two of you. What do you see in the drawing? In what way are the three relationships different from each other?" Caroline looks at her drawing and then at Marie and Martin.

Fig. 5: Relationship circles©

Marie says hesitantly: There is a space between the two in situation 1,"

"Correct," Caroline says, looking at a thoughtful Martin, who does not seem as if he will say anything. "In such a relationship, much contact does not exist and as a result no exchanges. Everyone does their own thing. The same behavior is apparent in many leader groups that do not perform in the fashion of a team, the way they ought to do. Each person takes care of their individual area of responsibility without cooperating crosswise. Possibly this can give a satisfactory product within a narrow branch, but without any additional value emerging from synergy effects and judgements based on totality aspects." Caroline takes a deep breath.

"What happens in the second circle," Martin interrupts. "Do they do each other's work?"

"Quite possibly," Caroline says. "E.g. when a director whose place is up in the cockpit takes a position with his finger in the dough for the pastry, doing the kind of work assigned to the level beneath him. However, it can also be a different scenario. In situation 2, one of the persons transgresses the other's limits. It can be the limits of the project, but it can also be personal limits. As examples, if you have ambitions on behalf of someone else, or if you tell the other person how he or she is, without your being asked to do so, or if you take on yourself the responsibility for another person, or if you expose the other person to stress over a long period of time.

"Sometimes it is all right to coerce a little. The dividing line is a subtle one. If you appear domineering all the time, or you oblige others to compromise with their own fundamental values for rather long, like feeling their responsibility, orderliness, their philanthropic ideals or other current values they may have, this is bad practice. Does this make sense?"

Both of them acquiesce with a nod, seemingly beginning to lose concentration.

Caroline gives Martin a calm look and says to him in a soft voice, "I am confident you mean well, and are enthusiastic about the potential you see in Marie for development, but when you repeatedly say she must learn to make mistakes – without Marie herself sharing this desire, you cross beyond her personal limits." Marie holds her breath.

"This is not something Marie has said to me – it is something I have observed at the meeting here. Martin, you are good at judging other people. Did you not notice how Marie's shoulders became rigidly tense, when you talked about her roughly twelve minutes ago?"

"Ohh…yes!" Martin looks as if he means the opposite.

"If you like, the two of us can have a talk about it 1-1 – I can act as a sparring partner – for there are more efficient ways to develop Marie – and I know that is what you want," Caroline gives a friendly smile. Martin looks away yet nods again.

"Excellent, then I will continue. In situation 3, we see a healthy relationship. Both enjoy their own personal space. However, contact exists. The perimeters brush against each other tangentially. Here transfer of ideas and thoughts take place, creating synergy. A relationship of this kind needs great sensitivity as regards the other person's limits, as we cannot devise a formula for personal parameters. What is acceptable to one may transgress the limits of another. We have witnessed this in the MeToo movement particularly. We can easily find episodes the newspapers have reported which some women felt was a violation of their privacy, whereas other women did not feel this way – and it still is a difficult task for men to understand the difference.

However, we cannot establish a formula. We need to rely on our sensitivity. Perhaps, Martin, if you used the same words to Anna about making mistakes, they might not sound as unacceptable in her ears. But they do so to Marie.

It will be a difficult job in the future to function as a leader if you do make use of your sensitivity – and the future has already arrived. Only it is unequally distributed.

After the meeting, Marie feels a relief. Both because the meeting she had been so nervous about had been a success, in a constructive and relatively informal atmosphere and because Caroline had helped her to demarcate a limit for her personality. It had also given rise to thoughts in Marie about what her personal limits are. It is not because she refuses to compromise, we have to do so sometimes, but because of her curiosity to understand her limits more fully and avoid unnecessarily crossing over them so much that she ends up again loosing herself.

ELEVEN

Top values

In the meantime, while she waits for her next conversation with Caroline, Marie devotes many of her thoughts to her limits. What is it that plays an important role for her? Why? She looks at the list with signals and starts probing into which situations activate them. One of the things Caroline and she used the list for is to analyze, how she was feeling that day in October, when they judged she was overstressed. Now she is less stressed, but her situation can vary – and situations arise that drain away her energy and relegate her to the fragile state of mind or closer to it…

On her next visit to Caroline, Marie tells her about the reflections she has had.

"It is coincidental, that you bring these thoughts with you right now, since I want to initiate you into the use of one of my favorite tools to wit, the Values-lighthouse," Caroline says, laying some papers in front of Marie. Marie begins reading them.

"But before you start reading, I would like to explain to you some things about it." Caroline looks over the top of her glasses at Marie, who lays down the papers.

"I'm ready," Marie says and looks Caroline in the face.

"Perfect, as a lighthouse can also help you, when you don't know how to act, what decision to make or which path to follow. It can help you to find meaning and direction in your life. If you do not know, what your top three personal values are, you can discover them now. When you have discovered your top three personal values, then you have a lighthouse with values to help you to navigate. This can be useful especially after experiences in which you have lost some contact with yourself, as you have done, when you have been over-stressed too long. Every time you feel a doubt, you can look toward the lighthouse," Caroline says and looks attentively at Marie.

"Hmmm, that makes me think of something," Marie says and places her hand over her mouth.

"Perhaps it is one of the lighthouse drawings that I painted with a couple of your leaders, and we hung it up at the office, not-withstanding they don't normally paint drawings," Caroline says, smiling broadly.

"Oh, that's what it is," Marie says with a smile. "Uma hung it."

"Precisely. I know that for many their lighthouse has become an important help as to how they navigate through their lives. The lighthouse can be of great assistance when you are in doubt about something. It can also help in times when the waves are in full swell, and the current is swift. Then the lighthouse can help guide you to keep to your own set of values, both at your workplace and within your private sphere, and when you have to make complex decisions at leadership level," Caroline says and gives Marie a pencil and a sheet of paper.

"That makes sense," Marie says and picks up the pencil and paper. She can almost guess she will need them to do an exercise.

"Do you know what your three most important personal values are?" Caroline then asks.

Marie straightens up. "I do have personal values, and I attach great importance to having a set of values, but when you throw your question at me in that way, I can't on the spur of the moment answer and say which three values I prioritize highest."

"That's how many people are," Caroline says, "so let us find out, what your top three priorities are. You have twenty minutes to do the exercise.

"The most effective leaders have a personal presence built on authenticity and values. Their reputation is not created by 'manufacturing' an image but by instead, embracing all of themselves, flaws included."

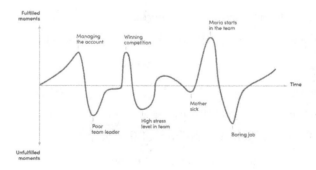

Fig. 6: Success Lifeline

Looking at your lifeline – a visual representation of the times when you are the most and least fulfilled in life – can help you gain access to authentic information about yourself: your personality, strengths, and core values. Only when you live accordingly to your authentic self and values, you can live a life where you really feel successful.

The horizontal axis represents your life's timeline (focus on span of time between your teenage years to present day).

The vertical axis represents your level of fulfilment during a certain point in time. Creating your lifeline gives you an opportunity to identify:

1. The things that fulfil you
2. Your core values.

Rather than being all things to all people, great leaders know what they are like at their best and bring that self to the foreground when it matters most.

On a piece of paper (or more), draw your personal lifeline to show how your fulfilment has varied throughout your life (starting around your teenage years). Your highest elements should represent your happiest and most fulfilling times: your lowest elements, frustrating and empty times. Label the peaks with the moment in time. Please note: If you have had a particularly raw tragedy, feel free to omit this period of time from your graph as it will not add to this process for you to relive something of this nature. Save your lifeline to look at it for the next exercise and bring it with you to your next coaching session too.

Caroline continues, "I will give this exercise to you, so you can bring it home and do it for the next session. "After you have done your success lifeline as well as you can, you can then analyze the essence. If something makes a strong feeling arise in your stomach, this indicates that it has importance. It can inspire you to choose your values. For some people, how to rank their values can need a long time. Speaking generally, you would like to possess most of the values."

10th Tool: Top 3 values

Caroline looks seriously at Marie. "Now it is time for you to find your top three values. Choose a high on your lifeline. Try and capture words, images, and general thoughts that stand out for you while you are at your best. Write it down here, in your notebook or on a blank sheet of paper."

"What words would others use to describe you at your peaks (highs)? How do you look and sound to them? How would they describe the impact you have"?

"Looking at your lows, what happens to your values and personality at these times? What values might be missing? Do any of your strengths become a weakness"?

Marie listens, nods her head and jots down with intensity in silence.

"Reflecting on the above questions, what are 2 or 3 top values that are most important to you"?

"On the paper I gave you earlier, which you can freely make use of, there is a list of values for inspiration, if you choose to take the next step in the exercise and identify your top three values. It is often difficult not to include but to exclude. What are your three top values? Should you choose one, that is more important than the others, which one is it? Make use of the list for inspiration..

"You may also choose values that do not appear on the list as yet." Caroline points at the paper in front of Marie. On it are the words:

Altruism	Freedom	Learning
Ambition	Leisure	Might
Recognition	Togetherness	Compassion
Responsibility	Generosity	Environment
Inheritance	Happiness	Courage
Authenticity	Harmony	Nature
Balance	Hierarchy	Curiosity
Contribute	Home	Mercy
Useful	Team spirit	Care
Diversity	Humor	Ingenuity
Effectiveness	Hope	Achievement
Simplicity	Initiative	Optimism
Ethics	Inclusion	Order
Adventure	Integrity	Passion
Fairness	Intuition	Patriotism
Family	Creativity	Reliability
Financial	Quality	Relations
Flexibility	Love	Respect
Understanding	Leadership	Justice
Parentage	Equality	Wealth
Peace	Loyalty	Cooperation

Truth	Vulnerability	Unique
Self-discipline	Gratitude	Tenacity
Self-respect	Team work	Friendliness
Self-worth	Time	Friendship
Security	Contentment	Knowledge
Equanimity	Satisfaction	Wisdom
Fun	Forgiveness	Vision
Beauty	Trust	Growth
Thrift	Tradition	Dignity
Spirituality	Well-being	Meekness
Stability	Faith	Honesty
Pride	Patience	Frankne
Success	Independence	
Health	Development	

Marie returns for the next session. They are sitting at the large meeting table. Caroline asks.

"How have you been?"

Marie takes a sip of her coffee before she replies: "It has really been interesting to do the exercise, and I have found three the top values which are mine," Marie says with a big smile. "And I can in fact feel it is important for me to keep them intact. I believe too I will get my lighthouse painted," Marie says with a grin.

"What are they? I am very curious." Caroline seats herself and looks expectantly at Marie.

"They are compassion, integrity and responsibility." She points her gaze directly at Caroline. "I cannot disregard them. At least, not anymore."

"I knew as much, and I believe, one of the things that have really used up your energy and nudged you over in the red zone is when Martin drained away the energy from your team," Caroline says.

"Yes, you are right, and I have decided to really keep to them even more, to not assume an exaggerated responsibility and try to compensate – since it drains me. Rather, by giving my team some of the same tools that I have benefitted so much from." Marie smiles.

"Caroline," Marie says.

"Yes!"

"Could you come and do a workshop with my team, and teach them some of the same tools, so they can retain their energy and thrive?" Marie asks with a big smile.

"Yes, of course," Caroline says with a smile.

"Let's plan for that on a separate meeting. This time is your time. So, let's conclude this session by I ask you: What do you want to take with you from this session? What has resonated with you?"

Marie replies promptly: "Having my values clearly set I can start living by them. I know now that if I compromise on them, it will drain me on the long run. Of course, sometimes I need to make compromises, but now I know; if those compromises are too big it will tear me apart."

TWELVE

Managing Team Energy

Marie stands looking across the meeting room. She feels agile. Every morning since the day she began doing *body scans*, she has meditated for ten minutes immediately after she brushes her teeth. She enjoys a good sleep and her long walks with her dog, Jax give her an opportunity to retire into herself and engage in reflective thought. This builds up her store of energy. Mostly, there is a good energy present at the meetings. Most in her own team. However, as soon as Martin participates – or surprises by joining in, it feels as if all the energy seeps out of the room.

Notebooks and pens lie beside each chair, and Caroline has already designed several wall pamphlets, which she will use in discussions with Marie's team today. She just needs to append the final remark to the last pamphlet, then she can start.

Today will be a team day with Caroline. They will practice using some of the tools, and they need inspiration to start them off on their own and develop themselves so they can solve the problems at their work. This also makes matters easier for Marie, since from now on her new qualifications must show results in the team.

They have already started before time. They have begun discussing energy at the team meetings. They begin by rating their energy level on a scale of 1-10 – and they have agreed that if they feel the energy has left the meeting, they must face up to this and do something about it.

They have found a common tongue to talk about bad or good things without provoking lifted fingers, and the improved harmony in the team has revealed itself more visibly day by day.

"Well, are you going to talk more about feelings today?" Martin says, appearing suddenly in the doorway.

Marie almost hops out of her chair.

"I didn't see you," she says by way of apology and a trifle out of breath.

"Don't use too many hours on this, Marie. You need also to get some work finished today." He taps with his fingers on the glass door, and before Marie manages to answer him, he is gone again.

Marie gives a sigh. She counts to ten. Right now, she was in such a good mood. She goes over to the corner, where no one can see her and adopts the stance of a power pose. He must simply not get the opportunity to smash up her energy. Not today.

Marie casts a look over her team fifteen minutes later. Caroline is ready. Everyone has come, and a good atmosphere seems to be present. Thomas, Marie's trusted subordinate, confirms this to be the case.

"We have been standing by the coffee brewer and talking about how much we like the project meetings, or whatever it is they are called," Thomas says, looking at his other colleagues. Many nods in assent.

"Delightful." Marie says. "I am glad to hear that." She rests the palms of her hands on the table in front of her and leans forward. It remains for her only to purge from her body the last memory of the remarks Martin made. Today we will talk about team energy, and I have brought Caroline along, whom many of you know, to act as facilitator for the proceedings."

Caroline begins opening the workshop. After all the participants have arrived, she exhibits her first drawing, so all can get a look at it, and she then starts explaining the theme for the meeting. She elucidates the awareness matrix with the four mental states, which Marie knows well. All nod their heads in recognition of these mental states and can remember them from their own working life. They tell about their own experiences in order to illustrate these mental states.

Uma confesses bravely she can recognize that when she feels very much under pressure, she enters a narrow state and does not really hear what others say and can make mistakes. Others nod in recognition of this.

Fig. 3: The Awareness Matrix©, Campbell (2023).

After they finished exchanging their viewpoints concerning the four states of mind, they focus on the vertical axis of the energy diagram. Christian gets a sudden revelation concerning why there were so many that seemed worn out and succumbed to stress at the workplace where he had his job. They performed their work tasks full speed ahead, the one task after the other, without recuperative periods in between, and without time for rejuvenation.

"A professional athlete would never have acted in that manner," Caroline comments. "In the world of sport, it has been known for many years, that restitution is a decisive factor - it is interesting that it still has not yet become a part of the *high performance*-culture at many workplaces. It is just as important for you. It can be you need to use your brains and not your legs in a sprint. However, research workers at Cambridge University have measured that your brain uses 20 percent of your personal energy, and when we take into account Kleitman's[3] research on the need the brain has for pauses in its daily function, it seems clear that it is not only athletes who need restitution. We all do. Do you know about the concept of sleep phases?" Caroline looks at all and sundry in the team. Everyone nods in assent.

"It is Kleitman who has done the research that forms the basis of our knowledge today concerning sleep phases. Have you heard about *rest activity cycles*?" Caroline looks again at them all. This time all negate with a shake of the head.

"Kleitman himself found out that it is not only at night we have different sleep phases. It takes place also during the daytime. Our level of energy has a natural variation in the daytime. No one can contrive to work at full capacity the whole length of the day without this exacting a toll on his energy resources. The normal pattern is the curve goes upwards for 90 minutes, after which it goes down twenty minutes, after which it moves upwards again. The most efficient way to utilize your energy is by following your curve as much as it is possible. This corresponds to driving a car and optimizing the amount of petrol you use by driving in a steady manner. You can also drive in a way you use too much energy. Your personal energy is the fuel your brain has. For this reason, it is important to keep an eye on your individual and on your collective energy account – and the same way you keep a check on your money, you should do the same with your energy. At least you ought to keep an awareness of the level of your

---

3   Nathaniel Klieteman is for many perceived as the father of sleep research. He was the first scholar to concentrate entirely on sleep. He served on the faculty of the University of Chicago's Department of Physiology. His papers include notes, experiment data, drafts of articles and books, academic reprints, newspaper clippings, photographs, artifacts, and audio-visual recordings.

own and each other's energy. You have already begun to have aware-ness of the level of energy at your meetings. This is a good thing, since energy facilitates cooperation. You can be more innovative, and you thrive more. When on the other hand there is too little energy present, misunderstandings occur more easily, and you become stressed and demotivated more easily. Energy is such a decisive factor for our well-being and productivity that all top leaders ought to have it as a KPI[4] in their organizations. It lies on the shoulders of each of you to find some sources that give energy. You yourselves can make tests in connection with your work and discover precisely what gives energy to each of you, and what drains your energy away. The energy sources are not the same. Many recognize this beforehand, whereas others must make their discoveries. When we work with energy, it is with sustainable energy, and this produces a lasting and stable level of energy. Consequently, sugar is not suitable. Some of the aspects research uncovers, and which in my experience are attainable and energy providing, are:

- 7.5 - 8.5 hours sleep every night
- A short stroll outside
- Healthy food
- Laughing from the heart
- Exercise and sport
- Short screen free pauses with mental rest in between meetings – even for two minutes

---

4   KPI is an abbreviation for key performance indicators. KPI's are being used in most large
     coorporations to measure performance. Each employee and departments get a set of KPI's
     to focus on. Withier they reach their KPI's are the measure of their success at the end of the
     year when revies and bonus are accounted for.

- The company of people with whom you work well or whose company you enjoy
- Not wasting mental energy on negative things you cannot change
- Work tasks match your brain capacity
- Your work has meaning or you feel part of a larger whole
- Finding your values and keeping them intact

"If I ask now you, what or who drains your energy away, and what or who increases your store of energy, would you be able to find answers?" Caroline looks at the team with interest. They all look at Caroline attentively. Their response is positive.

11th Tool: +/ - list

"I have left a notebook and a pen where you each sit, and you should now draw a line down the middle. On the one side of the line, you must write a minus. On the other side, you must write a plus. Now you must write a list of all the things and all the people that increase your energy store under the plus, and all the things and all the people that drain away your energy under the minus. For example, it can be:

- Special types of jobs, that increase or decrease your energy
- An activity like going for a five-minute stroll, that increases or decreases your energy
- Your relationship to some people, that increases or decreases your energy

Let's just spend twenty minutes, in which each of you sit with your plus- and minus-lists." Caroline looks out over the group, and they are already in full swing with drawing lines and writing minus and plus. She smiles.

After the exercise, they share some of what is on each other's list. For some in the team, the energy dissipaters in their lives are very salient, and this motivates them to do something about it. Now they can see it so distinctly on the paper. Black on white.

12ᵗʰ Tool: Power Barometer

Marie makes very frequent use of an exercise called the power barometer, and she knows it will be of good benefit to them here. In this manner she protects them too by teaching them what she knows and she thinks, "Oh," she says quietly to herself, "I can't quite refrain from taking on too much responsibility," She smiles. She is as she now is. That's okay.

"I have an exercise entitled Power Barometer. Caroline showed it to me, and I have gotten so much benefit from it that I have asked her to demonstrate it to you here today," Marie says.

"Of course," Caroline says, "because everyone can get an imaginary power barometer. It is a visualization of our sensations about our energy level. Perhaps it can look like a thermometer, a speedometer, or it can have another appearance. What is important is that, on a scale of 0 to 100, where 0 represents "low" and 100 represents "high", you can see where the red arrowhead is.

You can use the power barometer to check your present energy level, as well as your energy level in situations that are or have been especially difficult. I make use of this tool in many other situations as a kind of check-in for myself. With the aid of this tool, you can discern whether you need to do something to increase your energy store or find out what it is that is draining your energy away, if it is not obvious to you."

Caroline starts showing how to do the exercise.

"Can you evoke it?" she sends the question out in the room.

Several nod affirmatively.

"I see a thermometer like that, am I doing right?" Kristin, who is their new coordinator, asks.

"That's fine," Caroline says encouragingly and looks to see if there are others, who have something to tell.

"I find it not easy," Thomas says.

"That happens for some people, and it's perfectly normal. Sometimes it needs a little practice and repeat it a few times. In fact, I have experienced I keep deriving increasingly more benefit from the exercise," Caroline says. "I have something I would like to share with you. It is here." Caroline points at the slide show, where the text shows: it is a website address.

"It is a sound file, which is free and costs nothing, and all have access to it and can use it. On the sound file found at josefinecampbell.com, there is a short exercise to guide you in seeing your own energy barometer. Energy has a large influence on us, invisible to our eyes, but we can measure its effect. Energy is present in all of us and is present in how we interact with each other too. We do not need sparks in the air or potent chemical reactions to show us there are energy fields between people. A group or a team, just as you have also a common energy level, when you are together, or you can find yourselves in a common mental state, like being agile or hijacked, locked or tired, as Marie has told you about at an earlier team meeting. At a workplace, there is less freedom for you yourself to choose whom you will be in the same group with. You cannot change the others. However, you can alter your own experience of being together with others and change your own energy level, and as well your common energy level by your collective behavior. It consumes a great deal of energy to be negative, whereas you can host energy from grinning. In practice, it is not always easy. There is always someone, who requires more energy to be together with than with others. When an issue is unclear and in addition does not seem optimal, this can bring about friction, a feeling of lack of competence, conflicts, and power struggles. Such circumstances can hijack your brain. You lose your energy. You need to keep an eye on this. Therefore, the energy barometer is so good a tool to make check-ins."

The team meeting nears its end, and they make a common resolution to start all their internal meetings with a check-in on the energy barometer, before going on further. It is a huge success.

THIRTEEN

Authentic Leadership Presence

This is one of Marie's last sessions with Caroline.

"How do you feel?" Caroline asks Marie as she comes into the large meeting room.

"Great," comes the reply. The air smells fresh inside the room as Caroline just recently had opened the windows, and the sunlight shows its glance on the large silver lamp hanging over their heads. The lamp and Marie sparkle in unison. The two women sit facing each other.

"I can see it – you have done so well in this process. The most efficient leaders have a personal presence built on authenticity and values. Their reputation does not arise from 'manufacturing' an image but from embracing all of themselves, their flaws included. In the past few months, you have really built yourself up from the inside. Your building blocks have all been authentic pieces of yourself. Things that are true. It has not been easy. But look at you. You sparkle. The sparkle comes from inside of you. It is not just me who can see it. I hear you have been nominated for the talent pipeline."

Marie nods and smiles.

"I feel really content they can see me now. I also feel I have succeeded in creating an awareness of my core strengths, weaknesses, and values. I now realize the importance of a personal leadership presence and how it contributes to my success. I will go on reflecting on how well I live these values, and how much they reflect in my leadership presence. I know this is an ongoing process. I will continuously have to work with myself – especially when I have people like Martin around me. I may feel great now, but it has also been a week since he went off on a trip, and I know that the moment he is back he will have a draining effect on me. No one else but him can trigger me so much. When he is not around, there are fewer occasions when I potentially can feel hijacked and need to control my own behavior upfront. This uses up my energy. But it is worth it. Nevertheless, my self-awareness has contributed to my image regarding certain values and behavior within X-Corp. For example, the work I have done with the team on personal energy has spread like rings in water. I have people from other departments applying to come in my team and several of my peers have asked if I can help them with doing something similar. Oh Caroline, could you help them please?"

Marie glances at Caroline with a coy smile and pours tea from a silver pot into a cup. With a smile she chooses a tea bag from the fancy wooden box with different brands of tea on the table and continues:

"It is remarkable how my investment in my own personal development for surviving and managing Martin has correlated directly with my ability to influence and make an impact on other people in the organization, especially so in X-Corp where it is difficult to build individual relationships, because it is such a large organization. My personal presence has been crucial for my success as a leader and ultimately as an indicator of my growth trajectory. That places me now in a good position, which I most need. I had never imagined that this would happen – right at the moment when I was most vulnerable."

Caroline leans forward towards Marie, "Think about leaders whom you feel as having a strong presence. They likely aren't flawless or perfect, yet they feel comfortable and confident about their own abilities."

Marie nods and gives a sigh. It seems as if she has been restraining herself somewhat until now, as if her body until now had not grasped the fact that she is completely safe here and now. She is at Caroline's office. She is not at X-Corp. Marie takes a deep breath and exhales, enjoying the sweet smell of the green tea in her teacup. She shifts her position in the chair and her face seems to change composure. Her eyes open wide and the muscles around her cheeks relax. Her body is without movement. "Can you imagine all the wonders I could do for X-Corp and for other people, not to mention my own family, if I didn't have to spend soooo much energy on managing Martin? She pauses. "As regards my own future, I understand that as I progress in my career, my continuing to refine and evolve my leadership presence is the key to propelling myself upwards. Leaders with strong presence often:

- Lead with a genuine presence that is authentic.
- Use respect and trust within individual relationships to build up their influence.
- Are comfortable in their own skin and not afraid to share their challenges or fears.
- Avoid falling into the trap of trying to be all things for all people.

However, how can I do that when Martin is nearby. It is the opposite behavior of how I behave managing him. What I do when Martin is around is:

- Hide from him how I think or feel.
- Be as invisible as possible.
- Share as little information as I can.

"People who see me in both settings must think that I am two different people."

"Or maybe they just think that you are being smart the way you are managing Martin." Caroline contributes. "At least if they are senior people with experience. You would be surprised how many people have similar experiences like yourself. It seems almost as if managing a selfish boss is a litmus test in business life. Most vice-presidents I meet have more than thirty years of work experience, and if we discuss dark trait personality types like Martin, most of them nod and share their own experiences. Dark trait leadership is a topic that people just don't talk about very often. It is a tabu subject. Often there is a feeling of shame related to a feeling of being manipulated and being in such a vulnerable state of mind with a selfish leader like Martin.

The way it is for people in HR, who really should be the ones dealing with this matter, most of them do not feel ready to tackle a leader like Martin, and if they learn that his bad behavior is due to dark traits, many feel insecure and suggest the help of a psychiatrist. However, this they cannot get. How can you get such help? He was not subject to test when he was hired. I really think we have to progress beyond current practice and start dealing with problems of this kind. One obstacle is that we have so little science on this topic. Most experts write books on psychopathic leaders solely based on a single experience. We have very little science backing up dark trait leadership. Most deals with dark trait criminals. They can be made an object of study while in jail, giving them a break from boredom or a treat for their participating. It is harder to get data on dark trait leaders. How can you do it? Enter a corporation, and ask if there are any dark trait leaders wanting to participate in a study? They would laugh a bit at the thought of how that would result.

"Even though many experts agree that there is a difference between dark trait leaders and dark trait criminals, they still base their assumptions on the studies done on the criminals. A lot of it just doesn't match the reality I see in practice in corporations. This is especially true when it comes to what works and what doesn't work. It is as if people get too scared because of watching Hollywood movies and most experts say, just run. But I have seen several leaders who do not run. Leaders who do not want another selfish leader to determine when their career is changing over to stealth mode. Consequently, they manage them with proper support. Not everyone does this, and it does cost a lot of energy. But just look at you. You did it!"

"Yes. I am doing it. It is hard though."

Yes, it is! You feel bad every time you realize someone has manipulated you or misused you. It is a violation. They have too a way of finding people's buttons, and they trigger you all the time. They revel in this. They enjoy the rush or amusement it can give them from triggering other people. So, to avoid getting triggered, you have to confront your sore spots – you have to face up to your demons, so that they cannot be used against you to manipulate you. You have to assess your behavior when you feel you are triggered, where you become an over-responsible pleaser who wants to fix everything. Martin used this against you to manipulate you, and it brought you down. But now, you do not go down that road again. It can be tough to face up to your undesired behavior patterns, and realize how you really are, when you are hijacked. This needs courage. However, at the end of the day, do you want to be the only one who does not know how you feel when you are hijacked?

Caroline shakes her head gently.

"So how do you feel now that you faced all this?"

"Great! I feel strong now. Resilient too."

"It is of key importance that you continue nurturing your inner strength and that you keep an eye on how you live up to your top values: compassion, orderliness, and responsibility. Sometimes you have to compromise, but there is a limit as to how much you can compromise on these values. The work we have done here is not a one-off. On a frequent basis, which could be biannually or quarterly, you need to re-read the following five questions. Caroline passes a work sheet to Marie.

1. **How do I live according to my values?** It's important for me to seek opportunities that bring out the best in me. I am always willing to try something different and get a lot of satisfaction from adopting new ideas and turning them into action. I have a strong sense of potential opportunities and am always prepared to experiment with new or partially formed ideas.

2. **What behavior do I want to show more of?** Be curious about others, their perspective and what I can learn from it (especially when I am looking for a solution). Share my thinking more often to help broaden my network and visibility.

3. **How do I live following my truth?** How should I spend my time? Tell stories? Leave an impression?

4. **How am I when I am not at my best?** What behavior do I show? What do others find challenging about me? How do others regard me?

5. **How am I when I am at my best?** What are my qualities? What do others find compelling about me? How do I want others to regard me?

"… and you properly need to get other people's perspectives. Asking for feedback will be helpful for you." Caroline pauses. Then she continues: "What do you want to take with you from today's session?"

"This worksheet and a taller feeling." Marie says.

As she gets back to the office, she wonders how it all would have gone, if she had not had Caroline. She thinks about an old colleague, Uma, who also got sick with stress, and she never came back again. This happens to just too many people. She sighs. Now it is time to focus on getting things done, before picking up the children from practice.

FOURTEEN

How Marie Manages her Selfish Leader

Marie and Caroline sit in quiet for a moment in the middle of their last sessions, which X-Corp is paying for. Marie feels a kind of sadness.

"What you are saying is that there is a long way to go yet with Martin. He knows how to read people's minds and manipulate with us, but his sensibility is not very developed, and somewhere in his mind, he thinks perhaps it is ok not to respect our limits. In any case, he does not show any interest in self-development or changing his behavioral manner. I cannot change him. I can somehow manage him, but it is about how I manage myself, to manage him. Therefore, I need accept that I have to go on tackle him as he is, if I am to stay in my job," Marie says and looks a little downcast at Caroline. Caroline nods.

"Yes, I am definitely convinced of that too," she answers and straightens her large glasses. "It could also have been the case that he *only* had difficulty with controlling his impulses, and perhaps too lacked insight about himself, which can easily be the reason why a selfish leader behaves the way he does. He is not necessarily a full-blown psychopath. Whether or not Martin cares or is conscious of his behavior has no relevance in your situation. That he does not show a willingness to change is what you need to relate to. The big question is, will you – and how?"

"I do not intend to run away and just give up. I would like to handle this. I know after all the books I have read that this is in total conflict with what some psychologists recommend. It can be very harmful to work under a leader with so little conscience and empathy. However, the way things are, there are many of them in working life, and as soon as I advance upwards in the hierarchy, it becomes difficult to avoid meeting them. If I should give up my job every time, I encounter such a person, I would make no progress. I resigned from my previous job because of a leader like that, so now I want to learn to handle such a person. I will probably encounter someone like that again," Marie says and gives Caroline a disobedient look. In emphasis, she adopts a power pose, lifting her stretched arms above her head.

Caroline gives a nod and smiles. "It's a good thing, you don't just act submissively. Imagine, if everyone should change their jobs, every time they met up with a selfish leader, and just because of that. You have done a great job unlocking your authenticity and that has made you more resilient. Even though, you cannot be showing your authentic self, when you are with Martin it is still the core of you – and you know. Let's summarize your plan. We should use as a basis all that we have experienced works successfully in your relationship with Martin," Caroline says and gives the pen to Marie, who goes to the whiteboard and writes while Marie says aloud:

"Okay, it would be optimal if Martin and I could foster a healthy relationship with regard to cooperation, in which I could behave as I am in my relation to him, exchange ideas and have an openhearted relationship. If it were so, I would perhaps have more courage to make mistakes, just as he wants me to do. However, since things are the way things are now, and he constantly goes beyond my limits, I feel uncertainty – and honestly, I have not experienced anything other than to be portrayed in a negative way in front of Alfred and be mocked when I made a mistake. I do not know what his intentions are. There seems to be a big gap between himself and the real world. I cannot change him, though I would like to do so. The Marie you met a few months ago, would have taken the bulk of the responsibility on her shoulders, tried to compensate for the situation and struggle to maintain a healthy relationship, like your drawing with the circles illustrate in situation three. However, enjoying the healthy relationship in situation three needs an effort from both parties, and that a mutual sensitivity prevails to prevent incursion over each other's limits. I cannot and I need not bear the burden of this problem alone. It's Martin, who is my superior. He has the most say in this matter. It would be totally suicidal – and debilitating for my energy. This explains probably why I was completely fragile , when the two of us met the first time. I tried then at do all the right things, and I tried to please and to cooperate with him, as if there were a healthy relationship between us, but he has no respect for other people's limits – and he thinks mostly about his own self. To be realistic, what has an effect is, among other things:

1. To produce results – and to have documentation concerning my deliveries, that I can present in case there is doubt about my performance. This can be in the form of raw prints from our systems or short resumés from our meetings with all that has been agreed upon.

2. To have as little contact as possible with Martin, since he is a past master in the art of pushing my trigger points. It is like he can smell my past experiences and knows exactly how to manipulate me. My energy level must be so high, that I am *agile* when I need to have dealings with him.

3. I can adopt power poses, shake my whole body, walk around the building, and practice visualizing exercises and other things to increase my energy suddenly before I have to talk to him, if this is unavoidable. Just as I did for my Performance Review.

4. I need to smile at his ambitions on my behalf. Instead of feeling uneasy, I should remember he says what he does in his unfortunate manner because he wants to further my development – and when a leader wants to develop an employee, it is for him an investment. It is a compliment in some way or other.

5. Martin will sometimes try to distort the reality and gas light me or others. I need to choose one or two colleagues who I can trust do talk, and which whom I can share my reality so we can share notes and confirm each other's perspectives. We need to confirm eachothers reality not to loose it.

6. I can answer him point for point – short and clear and using as few words as possible. When he interrupts me, I must not let that floor me. I must just repeat my concise, well-prepared message and be ready to substantiate it with data if he voices a criticizing question.

7. I use my healthy sense of humor to laugh at him to myself. He is such a character. I sometimes think that he would have made a great character in a Hollywood movie. I just have to look at him that way – as if he was unreal.

8. It is most important that I keep myself mentally *agile*, so I can manage most things: Sleep is perhaps the most important thing. I must prepare for my sleep at night by lessening my activity and turning the lights down an hour before I go to bed. This includes that I must turn off all visual appliances so as not to bombard my brain with light. I need to sleep 7.5 – 8.5 hours. Although this sounds like a lot, it is in fact what I need – just like 96 percent of all other people.

9. In the morning, I must begin the day by doing something nice.

For David this means going for a run. For me it means sitting alone for five minutes with a cup of tea, before the others get out of bed and the bustle starts. In that way I start the day right.

- When I meditate, I improve my contact with my inner self – and my inner strength and authenticity grows. It becomes easier to follow my inner compass – and not let myself succumb to accept compromise with my top values so much again.

- As we agreed during our team workshop, we need to have some short breaks during our workday – as little as five-ten minutes once or twice a day – and I must have time in my calendar for focusing, so I can work with focusing without interruption.
- When I mostly eat healthy food, I get more energy. Green vegetables are always good to eat.
- My strolls with Jax in natural surroundings form a basis for me to replenish my energy, and I need to have time for them.
- Although I am not extrovert and do not replenish my energy in a group, there are persons whom I feel are close to me and contact with their energy gives me energy – and vice versa. It is important for me to enjoy good moments in the company of those I particularly care for.

"That became a mouthful," Marie says and looks at what she has written. She sits down leaning backwards with her hands folded behind her head. The sights and then she speaks clearly.

"Clearly a key here is that I keep on managing my personal energy and keeping connection to my authentic self, so Martin does not push me to places where I lose myself. What is ironic – is that even though I do everything I can to be authentic myself and others, I have to show a different face when I am around Martin, just because I am not safe around him. I wish it was otherwise. But it is not. It is my current reality. I alone cannot change the culture of X-Corp, but I can do what I can, to have a healthy culture in my team. That is my truth".

FIFTEEN

One more time

One and a half years after Marie lost her composure and burst into tears at her workplace, she quits her job. Martin, who is still Alfred's favorite shows distinct surprise, but quickly regains his composure. He more or less does not talk to her during the month she is still at work before her job change. Her colleagues on the other hand and her team are quite sorry, and two other employees have already found a new job during Marie's term of notice.

"I just don't want to remain here, when you are not here," Kristin says one day, while they stand by the coffee brewer. "Now Martin has unlimited sway. I don't dare stay." Marie looks at Kristin with surprise.

"Didn't you think we saw it? Kristin asks in surprise. "We all knew it."

Marie smiles and replies; "I am glad to hear you are remaining in the industry so we can meet again," Marie says instead. "Best of luck with your job."

Marie disappears inside her office. Susanne pops up in the doorway. Marie looks up. She had hoped for a little time to herself.

"I would like to hear if you have time for our exit interview?" Susanne asks.

"Yes, I do. Please take a seat." Marie points at the chair in front of her desk.

"Perhaps I would also like to hear if it was on account of Martin, you have resigned," Susanne says at last, a little cautiously after discussing the administrative details concerned with Marie's resignation.

"Partly. The plan you launched with Caroline has worked. I have found a way to make it work, and I have become a much hardier version of my former self. I feel almost as if I can solve all problems now. Martin has also lost interest for nursing ambitions on my behalf, and this gives breathing space. However, there is a big "but". I have lost more and more energy, and I can feel the loss. I find it very difficult to have so many restraints on oneself and all the time to be on guard. Therefore, I chose at last to resign, after I received the offer of a new job. A new job in which I could just be myself – without being on guard and restraining myself. Yes, I simply just could not refuse." Marie smiles and looks a little shyly at Susanne.

"Yes, you have done so well with handling Martin – yet, it will never become a good experience to have him," Susanne answers, scratching with her fingernail.

"All I want is to wake up feeling with energy every morning," Marie says, ending their conversation.

Marie still has contact with Caroline sometimes. A couple of months have passed for her in the new job. Marie has just paid a visit to Caroline for a brief talk.

"What is the new job like?" Caroline says and surveys Marie with interest.

"Good. I knew my new director, Christopher, from before, and he is decidedly not a psychopath. In the introductory phase of my new job, they gave me comparative descriptions for the expectations I should have to the tasks, challenges, and job roles. They told me in advance about all the difficult and hard things, which were a part of the job. However, Christopher overlooked a single thing. He does not know better. Would you believe it, one of my new colleagues in the leader group really seems to be a psychopath. Yes, you have trained me well so I can spot them," Marie says with a smile.

"It can't be true," Caroline gives a sigh.

"That's a great pity, since then the leader group cannot function – and that it does not do either. Trust is a missing quality, we cannot talk openly, and they are in progress with an absurd development concerned with psychological security. However, I keep hanging on. Psychological security is for sure an important thing," Marie says, "but it makes no sense to work with it, when we have such a person in the group. At least, I know now, what attitude I must maintain, so I am not the one to falter. However, it hurts to look on – again."

Author Bio

 **Josefine Campbell** is an executive coach and founder of Campbell Co, a top leadership development consulting firm for multinational companies. Campbell inspires and coaches leaders, teams and talents in large organizations such as McDonald's, Deloitte, Maersk, Novo Nordisk, and Carlsberg Group. Her approach combines the practical and the pragmatic. A four-time jiu jitsu champion, she is particularly interested in developing personal leadership in difficult circumstances, such as is often the case in modern work life.

Previously, Campbell was a serial entrepreneur and an external lecturer at Copenhagen Business School.

Her first book, published by Armin Lear Press in 2023, is *Power Barometer: Manage Personal Energy for Business Success.*

List of references

Babiak, P., & Hare, R. D. (2006). Snakes in suits: When psychopaths go to work. Regan Books/Harper Collins Publishers.

Babiak, P., Neumann, C. S., & Hare, R. D. (2010). Corporate psychopathy: Talking the walk. *Behavioral Sciences & the Law, 28*(2), 174–193.

Barrett, Lisa Feldman. 2018. *How Emotions Are Made*. London, England: Pan Books.

Barelds, Dick & Wisse, Barbara & Sanders, Stacey & Laurijssen, L. (2018). No Regard for Those Who Need It: The Moderating Role of Follower Self-Esteem in the Relationship Between Leader Psychopathy and Leader Self-Serving Behavior. Frontiers in Psychology. 9. 1281. 10.3389/fpsyg.2018.01281.

Brené Brown. *Dare to Lead – Brave Work. Tough Conversations. Whole Hearts*, Ebury Publishing, London

Campbell, Josefine (2023), Power Barometer, manage personal energy not just time and money, Armin Lear Publishing, USA

Campbell, Josefine (2020), Er du klar eller kapret? Bliv bedre til at samarbejde, lede og blive ledt, with the English title; Are You Ready or Hijacked? Become Better at Collaborating, Leading, and Being Lead. Forlaget Zara, Roskilde, Denmark

Cuddy, Amy et.al. (2010), Brief Nonverbal Displays Affect Neuroendocrine Levels and Risk Tolerance. Udgivet i *Psychological Sceince Journal,* Vol 21(10), DOI: 10.1177/0956797610383437.

Kingston, Marie og Malene Friis Andersen (2016), Stop stress – håndbog for ledere, with the english title; Stop Stress – A Handbook for Leaders. Aarhus, Forlaget Klim

Kleitman, Nathaniel (1987), *Sleep and Wakefulness,* The University of Chicago Press, Chicago

Kleitman, Nathaniel (1982), Basic rest-activity cycle – 22 years later, *Journal of Sleep Research & Sleep Medicine*, Vol 5(4), pp. 311-317.

Landay, Karen & Harms, Peter & Crede, Marcus. (2018). Shall We Serve the Dark Lords? A Meta-Analytic Review of Psychopathy and Leadership. *Journal of Applied Psychology*. 104. 10.1037/apl0000357.

Lilienfeld, S.O., Waldman, I.D., Landfield, K., Watts, A.L., & Faschingbauer, T.R. (2012). Personality Processes And Individual Differences: Fearless Dominance and the U.S. Presidency: Implications of Psychopathic Personality Traits for Successful and Unsuccessful Political Leadership.

Lindeløv, J. K. (2012), Bruger vi kun 10% af hjernen? Videnskab.dk, viewed May 2023, with the English title; Do We Only Use 10% of the Brain?

Cynthia Mathieu, Craig S. Neumann, Robert D. Hare, Paul Babiak. 2014. A dark side of leadership: Corporate psychopathy and its influence on employee well-being and job satisfaction, Personality and Individual Differences, Volume 59, Pages 83-88

Rock, David (2009), *Your Brain at Work – Strategies for Overcoming Distraction, Regaining Focus, and Working Smarter All Day Long.* Harper Collins Publishers, New York

Matzau, Majken (2014), Rigtige mænd går også i sort – overlevelsesmanual til stressede mænd, with the English title; Real Men get Black-Outs too – a Survival Manual for Stressed out Men. Copenhagen, People's Press

Printed in the USA
CPSIA information can be obtained
at www.ICGtesting.com
CBHW020305171024
15901CB00052B/876